MANAGEMENT
AND THE
ACTIVITY TRAP

MANAGEMENT AND THE ACTIVITY TRAP

George S. Odiorne

HARPER & ROW, PUBLISHERS

NEW YORK, EVANSTON, SAN FRANCISCO,
LONDON

FIRST EDITION

Library of Congress Cataloging in Publication Data

Odiorne, George S
    Management and the activity trap.
    Includes bibliographical references.
    1. Management. I. Title.
HD38.025   658.4   73–14279
ISBN 0–06–013234–5

CONTENTS

PREFACE

This book is an analysis of managerial errors which sprout from an inability to live with change.

A few years back a large airplane company in California decided to get into the business of making very large airplanes. Top executives were sent out to get orders, and they did just that. But although the new plane was radically different in design from earlier models which had been profitable, the old cost estimates were used. When one of their cost accountants added up all of the costs entailed in producing the planes the executives had sold, he discovered they had drastically underpriced the plane. He checked his work carefully. If the company produced and sold at that price, it would lose large sums of money. He told the vice-presidents of his findings, assuming they would appreciate his efforts to keep the company from going broke.

The cost accountant was in for a rude shock. They fired him.

It wasn't just a case of beheading the bearer of ill tidings. The vice-presidents were sure he was wrong. For one thing, everyone *knew* that the plane could be produced at a cost lower than his figures indicated. For another, even if he was right, they could recoup their losses with high volume. Too bad for that shiny-pants bookkeeper who couldn't mind his own business and keep his stupid little criticisms to himself. But he wouldn't be around any more.

The upshot was that the company lost $300 million before

somebody came in and finally sacked the whole top executive staff.

Of what use, the reader may ask, is a catalogue of ineptitude? After all, hindsight makes anyone a genius, particularly if he is not in the gladiatorial pit, battling for his own life. How jolly it must have been for the patricians sitting in their boxes at the Colosseum to chatter about how the combatants employed their tridents and swords, and the scribe to record tart comments about this man's background or that man's footwork. The stands of every stadium are filled with "quarterbacks" and "coaches" who urge the team to "go for it" on fourth and one. Any creature in the bleachers can verbally flagellate the outfielders who lost that "easy" fly ball in the sun.

The business world is no different. Everyone is familiar with the clerk at the water cooler who knows all about how the company should market the new product or fend off the corporate merger attempt by a raider. Universities are full of thirty-year-old experts with Ph.D. degrees who know what billion dollar corporations should have done about Ralph Nader, the SST, or the weak content of advertising campaigns.

Once, at the University of Michigan, a young doctoral candidate proposed a topic for his doctoral dissertation.

"I intend to prove the stupidity of conventional and traditional management methods," he told me.

"How do you know in advance that they are stupid?"

"Why, I've done six research studies using questionnaires and interviews, and processed the data in computers, and every study I have done has shown management to be stupid."

"I'll make you a bet," I said. "Every study you do will probably prove the same thing *because you've designed them that way.*"

Instead of wasting his energies—and valuable computer time —on an absurd and self-defeating premise, this young man should have been looking for ways to make management slightly more professional by reviewing mistakes with understanding, toleration, and even a certain amount of humor.

Errors are common, which is to say human, and therefore aren't too difficult to find if one looks. Is there any point to spreading everything out in detailed and organized fashion for everyone to see? Yes, for the true professional can learn from mistakes.

The major task of this book is to point up a common root cause of errors in the management of change: the Activity Trap—how to avoid it, and how to get out if once in.

It is important that we scrutinize leadership practices in business and government, in schools, homes, and institutions, in order to point out shortcomings and perhaps suggest improvements.

We may be able to teach young people who aspire to management jobs that mistakes are not uncommon but can be avoided if we learn from the experience of others. Peter Drucker has listed the three most important concerns of management for the seventies as (1) making better decisions, (2) operating at a profit in the face of changes in values, technology, labor costs, and foreign competition, and (3) training young managers. Perhaps this book can be of assistance.

G. S. O.

Salt Lake City
1973

Chapter 1

The Activity Trap

People tend to become so engrossed in activity that they lose sight of its purpose.

As THE WORLD GROWS more densely populated and human relationships become more complicated, reality becomes more elusive. As education enhances skills and learning, knowledge itself appears more ambiguous, and the need for simplifying concepts increases. The *systems* approach is a simplifying explanatory device.

THE SYSTEMS APPROACH

The public has been told again and again that when the systems concept that lies behind the engineering and scientific effort that put a man on the moon is applied to urban pollution, traffic safety, and business-management problems, all of our ills will be a thing of the past.[1] *

What the systems approach purports to do may seem pre-

* Notes begin on page 177.

1

sumptuous: it concedes complexity in the world but nevertheless seeks to reduce everything to problems that can be solved. Of course, there have been other attempts at clarification of vast amounts of data. Darwin's *Origin of Species* was one. Hegel in his dialectic[2] produced a general statement of the way things are. The scientific method is another kind of ultimate explanation of everything. Others are the various systems of logic, from Aristotle's syllogism to the symbolic logic of the modern mathematician-philosopher Wittgenstein. In limited areas Frederick Jackson Turner has explained the American character, and so has David Riesman. The existentialists have developed a system, namely, that no system exists.

Kenneth Boulding has suggested that there is not one kind of system but many, ranging from the single-celled organism to the transcendental systems (which simply means they are so complicated nobody can understand them). The search for a *master* system, a huge explanation machine that encompasses everything from flowers to factories, from microbes to managers, has ever tantalized the systems theorist.[3]

What most people refer to when they speak of the systems approach is the *cybernetic system*. The wall thermostat is an everyday example. The furnace consumes coal or oil or gas and generates heat, which is measured by a thermometer equipped with a special circuit. When the heat goes beyond a certain level, the thermostat signals the furnace to stop using fuel. If the temperature drops below a fixed level, it instructs the furnace to start working again. This is but one simple application of the cybernetic system. Intriguing indeed is the possibility that a somewhat more sophisticated model can explain a social system.[4] For example, it might explain a company, a school system, or a social club. Considering the enormous complexity of our social organizations, any explanation that would help us see and solve our problems, help people grow and be happier, would be welcome.

2

The *systems diagram* for cybernetic systems includes three major blocks, plus connecting lines.

Input   Activity   Output

Inputs are things that will be consumed, used up, or incorporated into the system. In a heating system they would include oil, gas, electricity, or more exotic forms of energy. One puts them in, therefore, they are called inputs. For a corporation, inputs are the resources required to start the business and keep it going—money or capital to buy land, erect buildings, purchase or fabricate equipment, design a product. Later, when the company is operating, it will need working capital to buy materials and supplies for cash, receivables from customers, and inventories. These resources are *committed* to the business, and when they finally come out, they will do so in a different form and a different time and place.

Activity is the second major component of the cybernetic system (the systems approach, for short). This is what people do to convert materials and supplies into more useful forms. The classical economists used to call this phase *production,* but it is much more than that. It entails engineering, designing, scientific research, accounting, legal work, traffic management, insurance, sales and marketing, as well as hundreds of subspecialties. The welter of activities which now exist and cluster together in special occupations has become enormous.

Output is the result of the process. It is the finished product or service, or the change which was sought when the process was initiated. If the process is worthwhile, the output must be more valuable than all of the resources which were consumed. In business, this *value added* is called *profit.* It is the basis of taxes levied and can be distributed in several directions. If the owners desire, they can plow it back into the business or they can distribute it as *dividends* to the people who supplied the initial inputs.

3

GENERAL APPLICATIONS OF SYSTEMS THINKING

It is easy to see how the model fits the business firm, and for some time economists have been using it to describe the economics of the firm. Over two hundred years ago, inputs were discussed under the heading "factors of production." What has not been so obvious is that a similar analysis could explain other organizations and institutions as well. School systems, for example, consume inputs, engage in activities, and presumably should have, as outputs, educated children with certain skills and values; but somehow this has not been happening. Inputs have been consumed in ever-larger quantities, but the quality of output has been pleasing fewer and fewer of the people who provide the inputs.

Governments apparently have fallen under the same kind of daemonic spell. The inputs they demand from the taxpayers keep going up and up, but in both quality and quantity the services they render seem to be deteriorating. The costs of federal, state, and local governments tripled during a recent decade. The ability of governments to consume vast amounts of the resources of the nation seems to the taxpayer to be almost limitless.[5]

Hospitals and other health services likewise make poor showings under this kind of scrutiny. The resources have been put in, the activity engaged in, but the average life span in this country is less than that in some other countries. Why should this be happening when so much money and manpower is being poured into our health care system?

Nor are social clubs exempt from similar troubles. Membership dues keep going up, as do time demands on the most active members: "Let's all get out and support old Joe in this activity because Joe has worked so hard in planning it." Yet ends can't be met, member apathy is rising, and more and more clubs

4

either go broke or simply lose the older and more desirable members.

Even the family seems to find itself caught in this systems dilemma. The resources it consumes are ever larger, but the output isn't what it should be. It seems that the old mechanics of living don't satisfy the kids any more. They insist that something different be in evidence—no specific ideas, mind you, just a feeling that things aren't very good as they are.

In business organizations, the amount of money being poured into research is rising astronomically, but outputs of new products are not rising correspondingly in volume or quality. Industry studies in pharmaceuticals, in medical supplies, and in petroleum have shown that products simply are not commensurate with the resources and efforts spent to locate and develop them.[6]

What Is Going Wrong?

Even when people are right in the heart of things, they find it difficult to understand why things are going awry. New ideas should be improving the system, but their unintended side effects are killing us. We design beautiful cars, and discover that they are emitting poisons into the air. We build picture-book campuses for our kids, only to discover that they hate the places enough to want to burn most of them down. The cities are attracting people from the rural areas, but they are mostly minorities, while the more affluent whites are moving into the suburbs. The cities have become festering ghettos, exploding with social discontent, crime, and drug abuse.

Persons who habitually succeed seem to have a magic touch. Studies of differences between the successful and the unsuccessful have not yielded clear-cut results. Apparently there are no major personality differences between successful and unsuccessful executives—good men fail and ordinary men attain greatness.

The explanation does not appear to lie in differences in their background, such as having been properly bred and raised or having attended the better schools; many men of mean or ordinary backgrounds succeed and go on to greatness, while others from leading families and the most prestigious educational establishments fail and are buried in mediocrity.[7] The only apparent difference between successful and unsuccessful leaders is that the successful leaders are successful, and the unsuccessful leaders are unsuccessful!

To relate this tautological explanation to the systems approach may seem hard; however, once the explanation is couched in systems language, the problem is clear.

Most people get caught in the Activity Trap! They become so enmeshed in activity they lose sight of why they are doing it, and the activity becomes a false goal, an end in itself. Successful people never lose sight of their goals, the hoped-for outputs.

Like a design in the wallpaper which you cannot see until it is pointed out, the concept of the activity trap clarifies many things that have gone wrong and shows what we have to do to set them right. "Success is best explained by unremitting attention to purpose," stated Disraeli. The Koran advises "If you don't know where you are going, then any road will get you there."

Apparently there is a normal and natural tendency to begin with important, clear, ideal objectives but, in an amazingly short period of time, people may get so enmeshed in the activity of achieving their goals that they lose sight of them—the desired outputs—and never find them clearly again.

The most successful people are those who keep an eye on their hoped-for outputs—their objectives—while they carry on complex activities. If the objectives change, they are responsive in their behavior. The less successful people continue the same behavior, even after the goal has changed.

The purest (perhaps the only pure) act of leadership is goal-setting and getting others to accept this goal and work toward it. When John F. Kennedy in 1960 set a goal of placing a man on the moon by 1970, he was illustrating results-centered leadership. It commanded resources and activity without major complaints because it kindled the imaginations of millions of people.

Falling into the activity trap is not the result of stupidity. In fact, the most intelligent, highly educated people tend to be those most likely to become entrapped in interesting and complex activities. Having spent years mastering one class of activities, called a *profession*, they persist in practicing those activities, as learned, even when the objectives practically cry out for some other kind of behavior. The age of specialization has produced a generation of people who have learned to become *emotionally attached to irrelevancies*.

The relationship between activity-fanaticism and the waste of resources is clear. Activity, especially professional activity, becomes more and more costly, consuming more and more inputs that are less and less related to any kind of output. As the activity trap enmeshes a person, he regresses to a more dependent relationship with the input-providers. "You must keep on putting in resources as long as I keep asking for them. But you are not to ask what outputs you are receiving in return for I am a professional." This attitude turns the professionals into the *irresponsibles*. "I insist that you continue to provide all my needs, without question, for I am a professional and you are not. As a professional, I am entitled to consume inputs and behave thus." The rest of society must behave as the parents of such children and provide the inputs, with ever-decreasing rights to question their use.

It is our own past generosities that have trapped us. School-teachers have flatly refused to be appraised, insisting that parents and taxpayers have no professional qualifications to judge their efforts. It is only through voting against tax increases for

7

schools that the providers of inputs demonstrate their desires for different outputs.

The rise of staff departments has increased astronomically the overhead costs of doing business. Companies have gone bankrupt in times of prosperity, eaten from within by their own professionals, whose work has often been wholly unrelated to any production of visible outputs.

The activity traps also extend to supervisor-subordinate relationships. As an activity becomes entrenched, it tends to become more meaningful than the output—the position becomes more important to the holder than the reason for which the position was created. Superiors begin to enforce the activity upon subordinates for its own sake. Supervisory systems become the governance of activity rather than the direction of output. *Be active* is more important than *Produce my objectives*. Time cards, close supervision, and autocratic bosses are evidences of the grip of the activity trap. "But," wails the boss, "they have to be kept active!" Of course—but there are high-yield and low-yield activities, with the highest that which is most closely attuned to the actual product of the organization. The activity-centered supervisor is chiefly concerned with the volume of activities—looking busy is more important than being productive. He creates a network of managers through which the activities are conducted and reinforced. Of course, a set of manners for engaging in them becomes *de rigueur*.

The obsessions which follow the attachment to activity have awesome effects on the management of change. Old activities take on an air of respectability which militates against innovation. Procedures become stabilizers which assure that old activities will prevail. What started as a momentary lapse becomes a bad habit, then a procedure. Finally, it emerges as a form of religion. The activity cult becomes the prevailing culture, and those who would press for change, for creativity, for the attainment of the brilliant possibilities of the futurist world are

8

stopped by the activity-centered people who dominate the world.

The pervasiveness of the activity traps is formidable. It can come into existence in any institution. It affects people everywhere, with its effects often devastating; for, under hierarchical forms of organization that are activity-centered rather than result-centered, *people shrink.*

THE ACTIVITY TRAP IN BUSINESS ORGANIZATIONS

As a dominant institution in our society, the corporation has become a major influence for governing our activities and producing the activity-centered society. Products and the ways in which they are advertised embellish activity with an aura of social acceptance that is most difficult to defy or ignore. Families "go out for a ride" on Sunday afternoon; they stare endlessly at idiotic entertainment; they become enmeshed in consumer activity for its own sake. Conspicuous consumption becomes an activity in which one competes with his neighbors. Such effects upon the quality of life have been adequately described elsewhere.

But it is within the corporations themselves that the activity trap's most pernicious effects are produced, for it is there that millions of individuals find or lose satisfaction in their work. The people-shrinking effects will be described in the following chapter. But first we will examine the effects of the activity trap upon the corporation as a profit-making institution.[8]

In the best-run corporations more people are clear as to their objectives than in less well-run, less successful organizations.

When activity supplants output as the primary objectives of the firm or any of the units within it, resources (inputs) will be wasted. Human effort may continue at even higher levels than before. The definition of a fanatic might well be the in-

9

MANAGEMENT AND THE ACTIVITY TRAP

dividual who is so busy doing his work he doesn't have time to figure out what its purpose is. Millions of people go to their place of work every day and promptly disappear into their job descriptions (the phrase is Alan Harrington's). Some specifics:

Quality control directors behave as if the entire corporation were designed in order that they might shut it down periodically and hold up everything that has been made. Yet the company is criticized severely for the declining quality of its product.

Production people behave as if "getting the goods out the back door" were the reason for the company's existence; yet the product has defects in quality, is produced at the wrong time, in the wrong model, in short or long quantities, and costs more and more. The vaunted American productive ability is no match for that of German, Japanese, or even Latin American producers, for American workers insist upon more and more pay with less and less production. The accretions of staff and support people in production have resulted in factories in which there are more and more materials, managers, controllers, industrial engineers, quality assurance and personnel specialists than people making things, with the result that costs have risen astronomically.[9] A ton of steel made in Japan costs forty dollars a ton less than one made in California. Pharmaceutical products produced in Italy or Switzerland cost half of what they would cost if produced in Detroit or Chicago, and are made by work forces which would be unemployable in this country because of their low credentials.

Accountants behave as if the whole business were created so that they can produce accounting reports, a substantial portion of which are totally meaningless and useless to those for whom they are purportedly produced.

Computers have created a whole host of occupations staffed with people generating information which is substantially useless mumbo jumbo, costing ever-increasing amounts. New systems of data processing and Management Information Systems (MIS) produce costly information that yields no innovations

10

and few problem solutions. In the hands of a plethora of toy-buyers, the computer is a great plaything.

Personnel men wallow in the production of job-descriptions (i.e., descriptions of activities) and are unconcerned that the paper they produce merely reinforces and rewards continuation of activities that do not serve the goals of the firm. They engage in miscellaneous activities which relate neither to the needs of people nor to the business purposes for which the firm was founded.

Labor negotiators behave as if the reason for the firm's existence is to defeat union wishes and demands. They propose that the whole company be run in such a way that they can win their next trial by combat. The battles accelerate, thus assuring that even bigger battles will be forthcoming next year.

Advertising men start with exciting ideas and get them accepted through dramatic presentations, but within an astonishingly short period of time discover that the excitement is gone, the familiar copy and used art are good enough, and the old media are reliable. Art departments within the advertising agency produce art for the artist's sake, and hackneyed copy grows in frequency. Robert Townsend has suggested that a corporation fire its ad agency every five years. Such action, if needed, is required only because the activity of handling an account has become habitual and routine for a department caught in the activity trap.[10]

Sales managers enmeshed in the activity trap turn their energies to doing the same things they have done in the past, only faster. Frantic control systems to produce more calls per day, tighter control over the sales-reporting system, and highly emotional "motivation meetings" to generate more enthusiasm among salesmen take the place of orderly planning and high-yield marketing strategies. The number of items in the product line grows, while the revenue from the entire line comes from only ten to twenty percent of them. New items don't get introduced into the line, and old ones which are outmoded can't be removed. The slogan "There's no problem a little more volume won't solve" dominates the sales field, even as successful firms are defining goals and strategies more clearly and improving their performance steadily. This marketing myopia which has gripped many firms to their disadvantage, but persists nonetheless, has been described by Professor Theodore Levitt.[11]

The Dearth of Strategic Planning

The major contribution of the people at the top should be in strategic planning, in defining long-range goals, in answering questions such as: Where are we now? If we don't do anything differently, where will we be in five or ten years? Do we like the answer to that question? If not, what can we do about it? If the organization seems to be a mass of confusion, it is because the managers cling tightly to controlling operations, thereby leaving the strategic questions not only unanswered but unasked.[12]

Sound strategy starts with explicit and detailed information about the realities of the organization's present condition, after which advancement goals can be devised in the light of risks, problems, strengths, weaknesses, and opportunities. Such strategy is the responsibility of the top managers, far too many of whom are deeply engaged in supervising too much detail with the misguided notion that activity of itself will produce sound strategies.

Huddled atop this huge ball, trying to control all of its activity, are the general managers and officers of the firm. Closer to the purposes for which the firm was founded, engaged more often than others in defining operational goals and measuring actual outcomes against plans, they sit on the front porch and try to run the whole house.

The significance of data often becomes extremely difficult for them to grasp, for they are likely to be inundated by conflicting and mutually exclusive evidence.

12

As reality becomes difficult to comprehend, the establishment of new goals becomes complicated, and the top manager himself gets enmeshed in the coils of the activity trap. Founders of firms are often emotionally involved with past successes and overlook new requirements of the business. A large retail chain was stuck with a product line of five-and-dime items long after labor costs of selling had made it uneconomical. When the revered founder had started the chain prior to World War I, clerk's wages cost ten cents an hour. By 1965 the minimum wage was $1.50 per hour, and everyone else had abandoned such personal selling in favor of coin-operated dispensers. But the old man hung in there, and if the directors were saddened at his lamentable demise, the stockholders were enabled to engage in some quiet rejoicing that his successor moved in with lines of appliances and other profitable items which saved the company.

Pretending that things are different from what they are, founders assume certain qualities in the people who work under their mantle, and human relations in their organizations become more and more convoluted and unfathomable. They fasten upon a few activity-indicative numbers and watch those closely, only to find that the real significance of even these numbers eludes them. The old curmudgeon who started his career for twenty cents an hour in the midst of a depression behaves as if today's kids should want to embrace similar ungodly experiences as being invaluable. The old man spends his time trying to stamp out such modern amenities as coffee breaks, vacations, and days of sick leave. Everybody under forty treats him as a comic butt.

The lamentable outcome of the activity trap in corporations is that the purposes of the firm are subverted. The question "What are we in business for?" gets asked infrequently and accordingly is not answered as often or as successfully.

What afflicts the large corporation likewise afflicts the small, rapidly growing firm. When the scope of the business gets beyond the compass of the top man, it begins to deteriorate. For the small businessman to start his own business indicates a strong desire for independence—a desire to control his own destiny. Perhaps it was a technical development of his own devising or a special market opportunity that he seized and turned into a business. Success in this venture required that he not only know all of the activity which went on in his business but that in fact he himself actually perform it. As success crowns his efforts, his responsibilities grow to the point where they are beyond his ability to manage. He centers upon control devices rather than upon finding and developing people to manage operations for him. His early experience stands him in bad stead, and he is shortly caught in an activity trap that destroys him.

Faced with the destruction of what he has built with his own hands, he looks everywhere except to himself and his orientation to activity. Big business, big government, and big unions appear to be the villains who have done him in, and he becomes increasingly centered in his own activities. The statistics on small business failure show that only a fraction fail from acts of God or outsiders and that most fail rather from the effects of their own bad management.[13]

The explanation for this seemingly irrational behavior is perfectly clear. The founder of a new enterprise often goes through some early trauma. In the formative stages of the firm, he brought in partners and co-workers who struggled with him side by side in garret or garage to make things run. One day he discovered that he was being betrayed, and that some of his best friends and associates were conspiring to steal it all from him. In return he connived and pulled a few dirty tricks of his own. Litigation, family fights, and charges of fraud and deceit flowed freely. Hanky-panky abounded. Once the bloody victor emerges victorious, leaving the predatory cats behind, he is forever chary of anyone who would present a threat to his control,

14

real or imaginary. Forever after, no matter how big the company becomes, he has a constitutional aversion to delegation. If some young smart aleck out of Harvard, bursting with administrative practices lore acquired in those halls, pleads for "some responsibility and a job to do," he is henceforth to be viewed with suspicion, if not downright hostility. What is new is bad. What is old is therefore good. The firm now is very likely to have become larger than he himself can manage, yet he is incapable of releasing control of every detail. He knows more about accounting than his accountant, about engineering than his engineer. If his sons should join the firm, brimming with ideas and motivation, even they must be driven off and lashed into subservience. The old man is a victim of what Veblen called "trained incapacity." What began as an understandable shyness to change becomes habitual, and ultimately a religion.

The individual professional and the small professional firm, too, it is becoming equally apparent, are as often victimized by the activity trap as is the large corporation. The senior law partner or the managing partner of the CPA firm or small architect's office is as apt to be obsessed with activity as the top executives of the giant conglomerate, if not more so. The senior partner, after departing law school where he edited the law review and garnered honors galore, learned that he could outstrip everyone by his mastery of infinite amounts of detail. He could manipulate memories of codes and statutes, and carry the details of a merger of three eastern railroads in bankruptcy in his head, where ordinary minds faltered. This mastery of detail, his experience taught him, became his hidden weapon. As a senior partner of a giant law factory with four hundred members on the staff, he still demonstrates this mastery daily: he knows the details of the library, the case nook, the billable hour count and thousands of other tiny details. The fact that he need no longer bother doesn't deter him from such mastery.

15

The organization ends up with no true head, and the result is a rising level of inefficiency of legal practice administration, increased costs of legal services, and a corresponding decline in the availability of legal advice to larger segments of society for whom legal services are too highly priced. The trained incapacity of the lawyer bars him from delegation of less important tasks to subordinates, with the result that the top is overburdened, and the lesser ranks fail to learn from valuable experiences. With such experiences denied them, they fret, live with frustration and, if truly talented, leave the firm. In such firms, led and owned by professionals, the domination of the activities of the lower-level professionals is seen as the vital skill of the manager. Such an orientation is perhaps the greatest barrier to their growth in versatility, profit, and prestige.[14]

The Activity Trap In Other Organizations

While most of the examples outlined in this book deal with the corporation and the executive, the activity trap is by no means limited to business firms. It reaches into the home, the service club, schools and colleges, the church, and government. While each would be worth a book in itself, perhaps some examples will suffice.

The Activity Trap In the Home

Junior comes home from school with an object wrapped in a brown paper sack, ready to present it to his dad. It is, we learn, the product of several weeks' diligent effort in the compulsory manual training class (now called wood technology) and is a combination birdhouse and tie rack. If the miters and bevels are a bit less than a master cabinetmaker might produce, Junior is nonetheless proud of his handiwork and can hardly wait to show the fruits of his creative efforts to the head of the household.

16

"Want to see what I've made for you for Father's Day?" he inquires breathlessly. The old man glares balefully at his offspring.

"Why in hell don't you get a *haircut?*" is his response.

This sad tale is a product of the activity trap. The elder is vastly more concerned about activity and the style with which it is addressed than he is about the effects of that activity and style.

The home has become a place where the mechanics of living are more highly valued than the reasons for family formation and for living in general. Prompt seating at the dinner table is more important at 6:00 P.M. daily than any other issue in life. Dad should stay out of the kitchen prior to the serving of the meal, and report there promptly afterward for K.P. Every hour is to be accounted for, with tight control over activity the order of the day. Teen-age children learn the impressive powers of forty-year-old women who use the gimlet eye and supressive social-domination techniques to put down evidences of independence. Household routines often show a total lack of objectives and rules within which the subject child is to operate. As a result, parents don't get inside their children—they are on top of them.

If you haven't gotten inside your children in the first twelve or thirteen years, you never will, suggests Dr. E. James Anthony, a St. Louis psychoanalyst. Parental pushing, especially in the middle class, is part of the psychological attrition of adolescents, making them exhausted and bored, Dr. Anthony adds. Oldness, as seen by the adolescent, is coming earlier and earlier—the aging adolescent and the aging adult, it appears, have a lot in common. Both parent and child are engaged in a battle for independence, and both end up feeling that there are endless days with nothing to do. Dr. Anthony's solution is a direct appeal: "Get off their backs!"

Parents who don't let their mates and children know what is

17

expected of them or who do not show tolerance for alternative ways of attaining these goals perpetuate the activity trap and the problems attendant upon it. Homes then become much less than they could be in terms of the quality of life produced and of the men and women who are created and grow up there. The people themselves shrink in such an environment. While this situation is tolerable for some adults, it is intolerable for growing young people.

For many, the procedures proposed by Dr. Haim Ginott have provided a key. He does not propose an abandonment of the parental role but a change in the quality of relationships in the home. Parents, for example, should accept responsibility for setting standards of output for children and for establishing policy guides that include ranges of permissible behavior.

The need for goal-less activities in the home is often underestimated in the fervor to turn it into an activity trap. While the requirements of leadership in corporations may result in very few hours per day of goal-less activity for its own sake, such should not be the *modus operandi* of the family at home. Even in the meanest sweatshop, the employees are given time for midmorning and midafternoon breaks, at which they are expected to do nothing useful for the firm.

For too many families, one extreme or the other prevails. In some family units there is no planned and systematized statement of purpose; nobody (except Mom) is committed to any goals. There is no mutual acceptance of responsibility for contributing to the attainment of the goals of the home, and as such the family members get no ego satisfaction from goal attainment. But there is limitless time for goal-less activity. In fact, home is regarded by the children as exactly that: *purposeless*—with all support provided but with no commitments in return and, accordingly, with no ego reward, no sense of mastery or achievement.

For other families, it is usual never to have a moment of pur-

18

poseless activity. From the well-organized routine of the members' rush through the bathroom facilities and on to a scheduled breakfast and the meeting of bus and car schedules, the steady grind of lessons and classes and clubs and chauffeuring in the midafternoon goes on. Then come the cocktail parties, the rushed dinners, and the evenings of clubs and lodges or sororities, of study and workshops, all of which add up to a wholly activity-committed organization. Weekends, always a threat in such a home, are a tightly programmed series of tennis matches, sailing races, shopping tours, and countless other diversions to pack each moment with fun (which is a synonym for activity).

In either instance, it is the activity which has gripped the family and the home in which they live. When the children become teen-agers, it is often too late to turn the tide, but a movement toward a kind of middle ground is possible.

The Activity Trap on the Potomac

It has become increasingly apparent to the people of this country that they are saddled with a monstrous burden of government. Confidence in government has diminished; credibility is dropping. Many voters feel there is little to choose between the major parties, for not only has each its own limitations, but they have many others in common. One suspects that government is not really being managed and that a substantial amount of the activity which goes on in the name of the public's interest is in fact in the interest of no one except the doer of the task—and he is often bored.

Entire bureaus and departments of the Federal Government are superfluous and engaging in activity for its own sake, according to the senior employees. Yet attempts to eliminate, combine, or modify meet with almost incredible foot-dragging. President Johnson issued a directive in October 1965 calling for the implementation of program budgeting recommended by the

19

Hoover Commission in 1949, but its full application has been hampered by the inertia and silent resistance of the huge body politic of the Civil Service. The cries of protest against modification of a "merit system" which originated in a reaction to the spoils system in Andrew Jackson's day have been heart-rending beyond belief. The net result has been discrimination within the Federal Government while at the same time the government is policing the discriminatory practices in business— not a condition conducive to enhancing its own tarnished image.

In the monster of them all, the Department of Defense, numerous issues of public policy are determined by the dictates of the activity trap. The costs of new weapons, together with misuse of the department's vast funds in public relations programs to convince the public that it should spend at such rates, have produced a strong public mistrust of the military. In the Department of State, a large, entrenched bureaucracy, enmeshed in a network of professional activities, consumes resources while the foreign policy of the nation is set by a few men in the White House. Few career officers and employees at the State Department would disagree that the department has become a massive activity trap: custodian of buildings and programs overseas, collector of information from around the world without comprehension of the reality it imparts. The Department of Labor does many things that could be done more economically elsewhere in government: gathers statistics that could be better collected and managed in Commerce or even in Agriculture; operates check-writing and placement services that could be done better in Health, Education and Welfare; oversees a farm labor service perhaps better performed in Agriculture; maintains a women's bureau made obsolete by subsequent laws—such are the functions of an outmoded agency which hangs on tenaciously.

The pervasiveness of the activity trap is recognized by many people in Washington, and affirmative programs to introduce better-oriented management have appeared. President Richard M. Nixon's program to reorganize the branches of government, presented frankly in 1972 to stimulate discussion and lead to future action, is one such measure. The application of Programmed Planning Budgeting Systems (PPBS) throughout government may be another. The explicit adoption of Management by Objectives (MBO) in numerous agencies of government, such as the Internal Revenue Service, the Veterans' Administration, and the Department of Health, Education and Welfare, is evidence that the problem is recognized. Yet even when fully described, the activity trap has massive powers for resisting uprooting efforts because the silent majority of civil servants are comfortable in it. At the very least, they are unwilling to trade the devil they know for one they don't know.

The moral is that perceiving a problem isn't enough to solve it. There are good and dedicated people in government who recognize the problem.

THE ACTIVITY-CENTERED CHURCHES

With few exceptions, churches have seen their effectiveness decline, and with it their membership. If the members have not disappeared from view, their commitment has diminished. The explanation? The typical church is an activity trap. Having lost sight of the higher purposes for which it was originated, it now attempts to make up for this loss by an increased range of activities. Covered-dish suppers, basketball leagues, great books clubs, couples clubs, golden age societies, bird watchers, bazaars, and pageants without end clutter the programs of churches. How could one define the output which follows such activities? Why does a church have a basketball court and three kitchens? Is it in business to produce Wilt Chamberlains or perhaps Escoffiers?

In some demonstrations, attacks upon the number and

quality of such activities have come from within. Younger clergymen and seminarians, finding the suburban church especially likely to be activity-prone, have charged that the activities are mindless and perhaps even Godless diversions from the true purposes of the church. The responses to such attacks have been two-fold. (1) The professionals among church men, based for the most part at church headquarters or in seminaries, have moved the church into new social programs. Leaders of this movement, such as Harvey Cox and William Stringfellow, have not only insisted that the church have goals but that those goals differ from any that the church has traditionally assumed in the past. Products of this new social gospel approach have been the defense fund for Angela Davis, the lending of money to Black businesses, the sponsorship of draft-counseling centers. (2) Within the churches themselves, mainly at the parish and local congregation level, there has been a resurgence among laymen of commitment to the evangelical mission of the church. Whether general unacceptability of the social goals produced this increased commitment as an alternative or whether it is part of a general renewal of goals-centered programs, there has unquestionably been a recognition of the growth of the activity trap in the church.

The Alternatives

Some leaders avoid the activity trap by stressing the control of inputs. These are the accountants, the conservators, and the administrators in some agencies. They are the budgeters, the old-fashioned efficiency experts, the controllers. For them, administration is the prevention of *waste*, which in practice comes out as the prevention of *use*. Fortunately, these individuals are not typical, and under proper organization they are valuable because of their reminders of the input (resources) being consumed. One of them becomes dangerous only when he gets to the top or when his influence is inordinately high.

The six most efficacious factors in overcoming the activity trap, thereby revitalizing organizations, have been the following:

1. *Setting worthy goals.* For higher levels in large organizations, these are strategic goals, dealing with the basic direction and character of the organization. For operational levels and individuals, the goals are statements of conditions which will exist if the personnel are successful as members.

2. *Getting commitment from people.* What is required is not a personality trait but some assurance that the individual will produce specific outputs in a reasonable time frame, within defined constraints.

3. *Accepting responsibility* for the results of one's own behavior and, in leadership, for that of one's followers.

4. *Supporting and assisting* one's subordinates by providing the resources and moral support that will enable them to do their jobs.

5. *Imparting a sense of mastery and satisfactory self-image* to those who have behaved responsibly and produced up to their commitments.

6. *Relieving employees from goal pressures.* This is the final requirement of a sound, output-centered system. There must be provisions for goal-less activity for its own sake. The rest-break, the vacation, the protection of leisure hours, the security of the home for private endeavors—these are essential.

Chapter 2

<hr>

The People-Shrinker

<hr>

*People caught in the activity trap diminish
in capability.*

SOME OF THE MORE PERVASIVE STORIES about army life have to
do with the ingeniously sterile activities that sergeants invent
for privates. "Digging holes and filling them in again" typifies
the experiences of millions of men in their military careers,
especially as draftees in war time. Although such activity apparently has no useful outcome—none discernible, at least, by
most draftees—it does serve the sergeant, who is able to picture
the troubles which the energetic young men in his charge might
create if left wholly without activity. Complete inactivity, it is
widely recognized, causes people to shrink. The worst punishments are those which isolate people and give them absolutely
nothing to do. The prisons which inflict confinement to a
"hole" are considered the toughest, for that is enforced total
inactivity. Removed from sources of stimulation, the mind de-
teriorates. One form of brainwashing prisoners in the Korean
War was such a removal from stimuli, after which the introduction of steady propaganda came as a welcome relief and, on

24

some of the less durable personalities, made impressions wholly contrary to prior beliefs.

While, in general, activity is most certainly better than inactivity, *meaningless* activity has many of the same kinds of undesirable effects, in less severe form, as inactivity.

Thus, one might picture the forms of management or control applicable to humans as having several levels, the lowest being *forced inactivity*, a higher being *forced activity without meaning,* and the highest of all being *induced activity, i.e., activity for a meaningful goal.*[1]

A goal is essential for finding meaning in work, even when the goal itself is not of great moment. Indeed, if a particular effort is understood to be goal-related, the suppressive effects of a lowly or even undesirable goal upon the personalities of the people engaged in working toward it are diminished. The movie *Bridge on the River Kwai* dealt with a British regiment captured by the Japanese in Southeast Asia during World War II. Ordered by their captors to build a difficult and complex railroad bridge, the war prisoners, under orders from their own officers, pitched in. The work itself and the emergence of a tangible product had an energizing effect upon the prisoners, even though the product was designed to facilitate enemy operations. The *sense of achievement* that accompanies satisfaction with work has as its necessary prerequisite a goal to which responsible people have made some kind of commitment.[2]

Organizations which have become deeply enmeshed in the activity trap have inadvertently committed themselves to denying this sense of meaning and attainment, for they have omitted the systematic provision of goals. Although the omission is inadvertent, its effects upon many of the people in the organization are the same as if the enforcement of meaningless work were specifically intended. This is not to suggest that *all* of an employee's or manager's activity is meaningless or not aimed at explicit goals, for this would be an incredibly ineffec-

25

tive setup. Yet there is evidence that the following statement is true:

The average manager and subordinate manager left to their own devices will not be in agreement on what the subordinate's job objectives are.[3]

In an organization that concentrates control as close to the top as possible, rewards activity as being meritorious for its own sake, and ignores behavior that evidences subordinates' desires to set their own goals in innovative ways, there is a substantial loss of meaning in work. The reverse is also true. In organizations where the major emphasis is upon decentralized decisions, where the system encourages and rewards individuals to set goals and make commitments to them, people find significant meaning in their work. And such organizations are apt to be effective in attaining their overall objectives.[4]

Loss of meaning in work inevitably follows from the activity trap. A business is started to achieve some chartered purposes. Resources are assembled from a variety of sources, such as borrowings, stock sales, or savings. At this stage, to those launching the venture, the goals are usually clear, exciting, and important. New businesses are often characterized by people so excitedly pursuing the attainment of their purposes that hours and difficulties seem to mean nothing. Insufferable problems are tackled; unforeseen obstacles merely serve to turn on more energy and creativity. Everyone is engaging in activity which, in its inception, serves to carry the organization toward its objectives. Then, in an appallingly short period of time, the goals once clearly seen become obscured and ignored, but the activity remains the same and becomes an end in itself. For new employees the goals are not nearly so clear or important. Changing circumstances may make it imperative that the original goals be changed, but the activity persists and becomes a *false goal*. The false goal becomes a criterion for decision-making, and the decisions get progressively worse.

The activity trap is a self-feeding mechanism. Top management loses sight of its purposes and begins to enforce on subordinates activity controls which tend to become increasingly unrelated to any useful purpose. Meanwhile, all that activity is eating up resources (money, labor, materials) and producing less and less output. "Do it my way" becomes more important than "produce our objectives." Clerks work hard at turning out papers that nobody reads. Salesmen push hard to achieve more volume in lines that cannot yield much profit. Inspectors behave as if the whole purpose of the business was to give them a chance to shut everything down. Production men get tonnage out the back gate by shipping junk. Controllers save pennies by spending hundreds of dollars on control. Systems and procedures men introduce tighter controls which cost more than they could ever save. *Doing things right becomes more important than doing the right things.*

The input of professionals such as engineers goes up, and the output of the firm goes down. The solution suggested by the professionals is to add more professionals. One large steel company has what some of its managers call "acres of lawyers," which means that more and more opinions are forthcoming, practically all designed to prevent something from happening. Even if some of the things being prevented are bad, many of these professional men are taking in each other's laundry administratively, creating jobs and administrative hierarchies to generate more activity that becomes increasingly unrelated to the purposes for which the company was founded. An accounting department discovers that costs are rising and concludes that the solution lies in hiring ten more accountants.

The Loss of Purpose

The adverse effects of the activity trap are reflected in profits or whatever other outputs the organization was originally set up to yield. In the long run, the good people who work in such an organization *shrink*. Dr. Herbert Otto once stated that human potentiality is only ten percent utilized. There is considerable evidence that the failure of humans to produce more can in part be explained by that People-Shrinker, the activity trap.

Take any two persons, one the boss and the other a subordinate. Left to their own devices, chances are high that both have become so busily engaged in activity that they have lost sight of the purposes of much of this activity. Try this experiment:

Ask the superior to make a list of the major responsibilities of the subordinate and, for each area of responsibility, to define the outputs or hoped-for results.

Now ask the subordinate independently to do the same things for *his* job as he sees it: "What are your major areas of responsibility, and in each area of responsibility what results or outputs do you think the boss expects?"

The answers will differ. The results will look like this:

1. On regular, recurring, ongoing responsibilities, the average boss and subordinate, caught in the organization's activity trap, will fail to agree at a level of 25 percent.

2. As a result of the failure to agree on regular responsibilities, disagreement as to what *major problems* exist and should be solved will be at a level of 50 percent.

3. The worst result of all is the lack of agreement between boss and subordinate as to *what needs changing, improving, or modifying*: here they will fail to agree at a level of 90 percent.

So the environment may change, but the methods remain static. And the organization is crippled by a thousand acts of its own employees.

How "Shrunk" People Turn Organizations into Bureaucracies

The organization, having drained its employees of their zest, finds itself peopled with zombies. They *look* like real people.

They wear neckties and white shirts, they commute from places such as Greenwich or San Mateo. They read the *New York Times* or the *San Francisco Chronicle*. They attack their routines seriously, and with a will. They are real people in every way except one: they are unclear as to what they are trying to accomplish. And they redouble their energy in producing nothing every time a crisis emerges, which happens often. But they live with a sword hanging over them. They may be chastised or even fired for doing something wrong, when they didn't know what "right" was, exactly. They may be written up for failing to do something that they didn't know was part of their responsibility, or for doing something that wasn't.

It's like finding an opponent's sword sticking out of your chest, then discovering that a duel has been underway for ten minutes and that you have lost.

It's like running in a race with none of the contestants knowing how long it is to be. They can only wonder if it is time to sprint for the wire—it may be a hundred-yard dash or it may be the Boston Marathon.

It's like being hit by a falling tree, after which the axe man leans over your broken body to whisper TIMBER!

The effects are cumulative.

Because employees don't know the regular responsibilities of their positions (at least 25 percent of these responsibilities anyway), they are prone to being hit for failures ensuing from ignorance. This produces a hesitancy to discover problems, for the problem they discover may be attributed to their own shortcomings, which may be brought up suddenly, without warning. The idea of suggesting something new and innovative in such an environment is, of course, almost impossible.

The bigger the outfit, the worse it gets. The layers of organization heighten the effects of the activity trap. The further down people are in the organization, the more they shrink.

29

What Life Is Like in the Activity Trap—A Scenario

Take a president who wishes that his vice-president for sales would show more alertness and celerity in introducing certain new product lines. He, of course, doesn't come right out and *tell* the man that he wants it—or that he had better do it or he'll be fired. Such behavior toward an executive as important as the V.P. would be unthinkable—after all, look at the money the company is paying him. Of course, he could figure it all out for himself if he were the right sort of fellow or if he were clairvoyant or had a crystal ball.

Yet when he fails to perform at the desired level of output or to introduce change, he is rated lower, and certain blemishes appear on his reputation with the chief executive and the board of directors. The president may sigh to the board chairman: "Old Jim is a fine guy, and he has many strengths, but I get a bit tired at having to introduce all of the new lines almost by myself, single-handed. I wish he would get in step with these new programs."

Old Jim, on the other hand, hasn't the foggiest idea that the old man is keenly desirous of his introducing the new line. After all, he hasn't really given a clear-cut signal to move ahead, and they have never really talked it through very openly. So he continues to drive the sales force to produce high-volume sales in the old lines, some of which the accountant has been telling the old man are unprofitable.

Each regional sales manager has attuned himself to cues, hints, and tips which tell him what Old Jim really wants. They never really talk about objectives, only about methods. Procedures have become a lot more important than output. Indeed, the last act before bankruptcy will possibly be to write a new procedure. The systems department with its new sales analysis procedures is screaming bloody murder because the new reports aren't being turned in on time and are filled with mistakes.

Old Jim listens to his experts, and his monthly sales conference is filled with dire warnings about what will happen the next time a wrong report—or a late one—comes to his attention. Of course, there are some other problems as well. The personnel department reports that personnel rating forms haven't been coming in, the credit manager is crying for his quarterly credit reports from salesmen, and the product managers on two lines are saying plenty about the failure of salesmen to relate to new promotions.

In the plant, ten levels down from the chairman of the board, the foreman runs around the department engaging in *activity*. He walks ten miles a day. (In one company, they required foremen to carry pedometers in their pockets to be sure they were active.) *Keep moving* is often the major rule for foremen. They check and correct, check and correct, making certain that the engineered procedures are followed by the "instrumental men" working there. Salesmen are making ten calls a day and writing a report on each call, but if a really big deal comes along, the sales manager closes it himself because you really can't trust the salesmen. "All *they* do is collect alibis why the product won't sell." In the employment department they are still hiring college graduates; at the same time, in another wing, the engineering manager is laying off experienced engineers because of a cutback in business. The sales department turns orders over to the cost department, who turn down 20 percent as uneconomical, while the plant loses money because it is running at only 80 percent of capacity. Executive secretaries file forms from below which nobody ever reads; but these useless reports are late, the offenders are warned to get them in (to complete the files). The production superintendent spends six and one-half hours a day in writing reports or attending meetings.

Activity wins, output loses. Such is the scene in the activity trap.

The Effects of Meaningless Work

The loss of clarity of purpose produces numerous side effects that diminish the capacity of the workers. It encourages regression to earlier life stages where they behaved in an immature fashion.

Immature employees are a major product of the activity trap. Immaturity can best be understood by observing a child. He depends upon others for food, clothing, and protection from outside dangers as well as from the effects of his own behavior that could injure or destroy him. He learns that to touch hot things means getting burned, that to consume toxic substances can bring discomfort or worse. The parent is responsible for seeing that the needs of the child are met until such time as he is able to cope for himself.[5]

The rates at which children move to maturity are fairly predictable, even though the precocious may achieve self-reliance faster. One might contrast the characteristics of immaturity and maturity as follows:

Immaturity	*Maturity*
Lacks competence	Competent
Not responsible	Responsible
Dependent	Independent
Reckless	Thoughtful
Destructive	Constructive
Present-centered	Future-centered
Self-centered	Self-denial

To move from immaturity to maturity should be a fundamental goal for everyone, but under activity-centered management, the process is reversed. People move from maturity to immaturity.

32

Uncommitted employees are a second major product of the activity-centered organization. Because goals are apparently being deliberately obscured in the design of limited, repetitive jobs by the organization and the boss, the level of commitment is lowered. With no clear-cut target except to do the work put before them, the "emphasis shifts from attainment, achievement and results to job survival. Denied the excitement of pursuing ultimate objectives, shunted into work for its own sake, the employee feels himself dependent upon the *ex post facto* judgments of a superior as to whether or not success is to be his. His job behavior becomes apathetic and uninteresting; it is limited to a cluster of tasks encircled and protected by professional canons of behavior or a union contract and by a bureaucratic culture which keeps him within that circle."[6]

Competence becomes a matter of engaging in an elegant cluster of activities rather than of arriving at higher levels of output. The most competent person is the one who can execute the most complex and technically difficult array of activities with the least personal effort and the fewest errors in procedure and who does so with a certain amount of flair and *élan* which permits him to make the complicated task seem easy. Ability to reduce the time lost because of uncertainty and of having to redo activity is another evidence of professionalism. Finding easier ways to do things often permits the competent person to have extra minutes or hours of nonworking time within his workday, and he is likely to be smooth, easy, and relaxed in his movements and actions. Yet sadly missing are the concepts that *higher yields* should be the end result of competence and that competence should include ability to change *what* things are done.

In the activity-centered organization, it is entirely possible to improve competence without improving output.

33

APPARENT COMPETENCE OR REAL COMPETENCE?

The catch in improving competence in the activity-centered organization is that it is cosmetic in its effects. People move about with an air of busyness and seeming purposefulness. They check the Xerox against the master. They stride manfully from meeting to meeting carrying folders under their arms. Their horn-rimmed glasses and school ties exude quiet efficiency. At long conference tables they pose for "Holy Pictures" and utter the jargon of the graduate school of business, or they lean over drawings or walk about the plant with hard hats, and play out parodies of themselves. In one large engineering department the walls of the entry area are lined with Professional Engineering certificates. The startling thought occurred that perhaps this was absolutely essential since it was impossible to otherwise discern their professionalism in what they were *producing*.

On the other hand are those corporations where things get done, the products are made and delivered on time at suitable costs. General Electric, which has the happy problem of managing a growth of one billion dollars a year exudes such class, but they also produce like crazy. General Motors, the world's largest and still growing corporation, retains it leadership despite the fact that 40 percent of its managers never went to college, that it hires more blacks and disadvantaged people than other corporations, and that it violates many of the more cherished norms of other less successful corporations. Yet you'll rarely meet a manager or employee in that giant who isn't crystal clear as to the objectives of his job. That's no accident. It's their secret weapon.

Low levels of achievement motivation are present in an activity-centered organization. When work is considered not so much in terms of results and outputs but in the obvious evi-

34

dences of activity—hard work, sweat, long hours put in at the desk, resilience in taking on especially dirty jobs—achievement motivation is lost. Lost, too, in the process are the more meaningful evidences of achievement motivation, such as the acceptance of responsibility for higher outputs and greater levels of attainment in more work. The attainment of a high level of output and high achievement motivation requires the addition of meaning to the task. More effort or smarter effort is likely when a man discovers a visible connection to something which he can see is meaningful, relevant, and important to himself.[7]

Studies of Air Force trainees showed that when they could see that their training programs were related to their own subsequent survival, they performed better on a whole host of various achievement indicators, including morale, performance, vigor, and level of tension.[8]

At General Electric a comparative study was done of departments where specific, objectively defined work goals with some explicit yardsticks for performance were set, and of other departments where more activity-centered management performance reviews were customary. The company found that attitudes toward work were significantly better in the departments which centered themselves around goals. It was also found that the members of the goals-centered departments were much more likely to take specific action to improve performance than those of the departments where they were rated on their personalities, their efforts alone, or some other criteria not especially related to goals.[9]

Uncertainty about one's place in the organization is still another consequence of the activity trap. Called "role conflict" by the behavioral scientists, uncertainty lowers organizational effectiveness and the satisfaction of the individual, producing emotional strain, indecision, and other evidences of psychological conflict.[10] This conflict works against zestful application of energy toward the organization's goals, which requires that

35

the worker be relatively free of excessive frustration, anxiety, and dissatisfaction. While role conflict is apparently inherent in organization life, and is not limited to corporations, it can be diminished through direction toward goals. Frequently there will be conflicting goals, especially at the higher echelons.[11] Perhaps the greatest evil of all is the category of conflict that is management-produced and generated, and which is built unnecessarily into the management system and organization patterns of the company or institution.

While role conflict is inevitable, it can be diminished by systematic and frequent consultations between bosses and subordinates, open communication between groups, and explicit definition of expectations of subordinates by bosses and of cross-level groups with one another.

The Solemnity of the Absurd

In large organizations everywhere there are significant numbers of people for whom the absurd is a daily companion. The solemn character of activity for its own sake, competence without output, is both prevalent and, at the same time, preventable. This absurdity is born and fostered when a once-important goal has bred a cluster of activities, and then the goal disappears and the activities continue. Then another important goal is born and a new cluster of activities in another site is developed, and the two clusters of activities become mutually exclusive, self-canceling, and nullify one another. Yet each of the work groups engaging in the activities moves forward efficiently with the solemnity of the high priest, and their task assumes a religiosity in the minds of its devotees. Nothing apparently brings out the zeal and ardor of staff like clinging to an obsolete activity which is no longer related to any output of value.

The congregation that decided to build a new church, using

the bricks from the old one, was being sensible and competent. It evolved into the absurd when it amended that vote to declare that the old church would not be torn down until the new one was ready for services. Yet many company and government policies conform to such a model. The large insurance company that repaid tuition to people who took evening courses of benefit to the company was rewarded by a savings when one supervisor used his learning experience to reduce costs through eliminating three positions. Shortly afterward his pay was cut because he now had fewer people under his control. Protesting this absurdity, he was solemnly informed, "Sorry. That's policy."

At a large western university the administration invited the legislature to lunch, at which time they pleaded urgently for more money to advance wisdom. To insure that the solons would not have to walk too far, they were directed to park their cars in a nearby parking lot. During the impassioned speeches, a crew came along and installed parking meters, followed immediately by a meter maid who solemnly ticketed the entire state legislature's vehicles with fix-proof tickets that the legislature had recently created.

Activity-centered organizations are often rich in procedures. As John Gardner once said, "The last act of a dying civilization is that somebody will be writing a procedure." All of which may be perfectly sensible when the procedure was originally related to some meaningful goal and still serves that useful function. Yet, when conflicting procedures catch people in cruel squeezes, additional management responsibility to the people in the organization is needed. When a human being is caught between two logical procedures by some special and absurd circumstance, another human being with managerial responsibility must be empowered and trained to step in and make exceptions, thereby preserving the humanity of the organization. Goal-centered organizations in contrast with activity-centered organizations can make such adjustments. Schools of business and public administration need a new course to be called "When to break the rules and violate procedures to save somebody's soul."

Chapter 3

How Reality Becomes Invisible to the Board of Directors

The activity trap originates at the top of the organization and extends to the lower levels.

A NOTED ANTHROPOLOGIST, writing about procedures for investigating backward tribes, stated that his key rule always is to visit the chief first. A similar practice is wise in studying the corporation and other large organizations, for one must look at the leadership as the source of lost reality. In the large corporation, this is the fault of the board of directors, especially the chairman.

Their loss of touch with the realities of the organization cascades like a waterfall onto the executive ranks, thence onto the lower levels, where subordinates compensate for loss of direction by redoubling activity. Emotionally involved in their work, the purpose of which is now missing, they erect defenses against unsettling facts. They resist efforts (such as management information systems) to ferret them out, and instead attempt to make these systems justify their activities.

When I first was invited to join a board of directors, I was pleased to be asked to sit at the top level of a company and looked forward to the experience. I pitched in to learning about *the company, I asked questions at the meetings, and darned good ones. I often called the president between board meetings with suggestions and ideas. Much to my surprise, I wasn't re-elected at the next annual meeting, and all they told me was some kind of vague story about reorganizing to make place for a customer at their banker's suggestion. I now know that that wasn't the reason. It was because I was too active. Presidents don't want people on the board to try to run the company or be too assertive. I'm on several boards now, and generally I attend the meetings, give my opinion when it's asked for, and the rest of the time keep my mouth shut.*

This quotation seems to summarize the typical relationship of a member of the board of directors with the corporation. It highlights the painful situation in the head offices of corporations.

1. *The board of directors doesn't direct.* It endorses the recommendations of the officers, especially when the officers themselves comprise the membership of the board in whole or in part. Individual members may offer solicited advice in their own area of expertise; otherwise, rarely, if ever, do they intervene in mundane management. When it becomes necessary to find or remove a president, the board is responsible. It also serves as a "mirror" in which management views, preens, and disciplines itself. But it doesn't *direct*.[1]

2. *The board of directors isn't in touch with reality.* Customarily, the directors must avoid interfering or even being abrasive and unpleasant. Prying deeply into the details of the business is particularly frowned upon. The dilemma is simply this: if the director is going to direct, he must be reelected to the board (or recommended in the first place) and this will not occur if he is "troublesome"—that is, too inquisitive, assertive, probing, and judgmental about the affairs of the company. Yet if he is to find out what is really happening in the company, he

40

must upon occasion be probing, assertive, demanding, and judgmental.

The only way to become a member of a board of directors and to last as such is to avoid most of the realities in the firm.

The inside director, it may be assumed, will have more knowledge of the company than the outside director.[2] The president and the executive and group vice-presidents who sit on the board have company-wide knowledge of the business, but they also have a personal stake in not divulging all; that they know their objectivity is not beyond question. Although the reality he perceives is often in only a limited, special sphere such as finance or marketing, the inside director's limitations result less from his remoteness from reality than from his impotence. He is dependent upon the president and chairman for his livelihood and upon his peers for support in his area of responsibility.

BOARDS OF DIRECTORS UNDER FIRE

It is generally considered prestigious for a person to be a member of several corporate boards of directors. Often this prestige is supplemented by more tangible rewards: director's fees that amount to a fairly generous *per diem* for the member who attends meetings regularly, as well as worthwhile associations with other board members. Also, there may be opportunities to acquire invaluable knowledge—for instance, an officer in company A who sits on the board of company B can observe how the officers of company B function, how they solve their problems and view the future—in effect, a remunerative seminar arrangement.

Recently, however, expectations as to boards of directors have been rising. The pleasant aspects of directorship are increasingly being supplanted by onerous responsibilities. This trend has become evident in the publicity surrounding some widely noted

41

and perhaps scandalous events in certain corporations. As a result of these events, which have been rather frequent in recent years, many boards of directors are electing outside members who will assure that more searching questions are asked at the board level.[3]

Many analysts, government officials, and investors have wondered how the board of directors of the Penn Central Railroad could apparently have been so uninformed about the serious financial condition of the company prior to its bankruptcy. Months in advance there had been a steady drain on cash reserves, but the financial department is said not to have reported this to either the officers or the board, thus the somnolence of the board apparently went undisturbed.[4]

In lesser instances, too, it may be asked whether a board is carrying out its directorial responsibilities when the public, the stockholders, and the employees are hurt by management actions taken without review and approval by the board. The Internal Revenue Service is adamant on past-due taxes. The limitations on the personal liability of directors do not cover such taxes as employee withholding payments. Directors are personally and individually liable for the failure of corporations to make timely payments. Other examples of pressure on directors include increasing insistence on this liability for false statements and certifications—these have always been illegal, but this liability was scarcely noted in the past. More serious from a director's viewpoint are the number of instances in which boards have been sued for failure to perform their trustee functions with suitable care. As trustees, the directors are charged with certain responsibilities regarding corporate assets, and it is not uncommon now for discontented stockholders to sue the directors for misfeasance or nonfeasance in this role. Consumers have also been increasingly asserting their rights by bringing lawsuits against companies and officers and directors for failure of the product to function safely; more and more

42

frequently, they have been obtaining redress for damages. Ecology clubs, consumer activist groups, women's and gay liberation movements, and others have purchased stock in corporations and sent spokesmen to annual meetings to press the directors and officers for more favorable attitudes toward their group or some social cause, such as a boycott of South Africa. When directors find themselves in the glare of unaccustomed publicity, they are somewhat more inclined than usual to feel justified in probing into the inner details of the business.[5]

The most likely instrument of change with regard to boards of directors, however, is the Securities and Exchange Commission, which controls the issuance and sale of stocks and other securities. By means of its vital powers over the company's access to the investing public's funds, the SEC engages in quasi-legislative, quasi-judicial persuasion. Although the SEC seldom exercises it, the agency's control over boards of directors could be extensive. At the time of a new stock issue, it checks the personal backgrounds of members of the board, using information provided for the most part by the directors themselves. In an August 1972 speech in San Francisco that was reported as "wide-ranging in its application," SEC Chairman Casey indicated an intention to scrutinize policies and compositions of boards more closely in the future.[6]

The SEC's power might be extended to rules for the mix of inside and outside directors. The agency might stipulate the kinds of information with which boards of directors must be provided, and might require the board members to certify that they have read it. The SEC might implement compelling issues of public policy as those arise. For example, it is not beyond the realm of possibility that the SEC might require board membership to include minority-race representation or female representation where substantial numbers of such groups are substantially affected by the company's operation. After all, as

43

advocates of this possibility point out, if General Motors, the world's largest manufacturer, can have a black director, other corporations could, too; the presence of such representatives might even increase perception of reality in a board's deliberations.

Perhaps the best testimony to the increasing pressure upon boards of directors is the rise in the cost of premiums for directors' liability insurance. The traditional limitations on the personal liability of directors are more and more proving to be rather flimsy protection for them. Casualty companies that previously would insure directors as a matter of course against the unlikely event of judgments being rendered against them now will either refuse to do so or will charge exorbitant premiums. Corporate directors often find it prudent to consult an attorney as to the extent of their risks and liabilities before joining a board.

A lamentable conclusion might be that the very conditions which would bring the board of directors into touch with reality are those which are apt to drive good outside directors away. For to be in touch with reality entails responsibility for failure.

The moment of truth for a board comes with the selection of a president. Perhaps the board itself has removed the former president. However, such drastic action may not have been instigated by the board, but rather may result from a financial crisis, such as a large loan which is due and cannot be repaid. The bank, which is often represented on the board as a condition for granting a loan, agrees to extend the due date, but only on the condition that the management be changed. There really is no choice between survival of the company (if the note is called, bankruptcy follows) and firing the president and finding a replacement.

In other cases, the president retires and the board elects a new one. The outgoing president may have some say in selecting

44

his successor (although his wishes are not automatically granted) because he may have groomed one or more candidates, and he can best attest to their relative competence. If there is no suitable candidate from within the executive ranks, the onus shifts back to the board, which may engage a professional search firm and then judge its recommendations. Or the board may conduct its own search, thereby coming up against its limitations, namely, lack of knowledge of the details of the business. In hiring a president, however, these limitations are less severe than might be supposed.

The selection of a chief executive by a board reflects upon its own performance. The board of Curtis Publishing Company was not rated as outstanding by many of its observers, and a succession of presidents came and went. The demise of the *Saturday Evening Post*, a highly visible product, prompted a spate of books detailing the events leading to its death throes, thereby opening a window not ordinarily open to public eyes.[7] Threats of scandal and misdeameanors can likewise bring to light the actions of the board and its individual members. The Chrysler Corporation board of directors in 1961 actively fired the president, found a new one from within its own membership (George Love), and channeled the company into new lines. The changes brought outstanding success: a loss of forty million dollars was dramatically reversed by earnings of 186 million dollars the following year.[8]

THE ROLE OF DIRECTORS IN SETTING OBJECTIVES

While the role of the board in choosing a president is clear and is usually carried out with definite results, another directorial responsibility is frequently less well met, if at all. The vital function of setting corporate objectives is often not performed by the board but left to the officers and managers. The importance of objectives in shaping the character and functioning of the firm has been emphasized repeatedly in modern management literature.[9] When directors abdicate this function, they turn the future of the firm over to its officers.

The abandonment of the function of setting corporate objectives is the most serious consequence of the usual confusion of myth and reality by the board of directors.

Large corporations do not in fact operate without objectives, but these are most often set by their officers as a result of what amounts to serious nonfeasance on the part of their boards. While this dereliction is explainable, it cannot be justified. The following is a typical procedure for setting corporate goals:

1. The corporate officers, with the assistance of long-range planners, economists, engineers, accountants, and other members of their staff, define five-year (or some other multi-year) goals. For these they calculate probable financial consequences and budgets, including revenue and expense projection, program plans, and personal proposals.

2. Projections, especially those that require budgetary commitments and heavy debt financing or equity financing, are brought to the board for their approval. Because of the character of the relationship which the officers have established with the board and also because of the pressures upon individual members to avoid any semblance of interference in the detailed operation of the business, the directors will ordinarily accept the objectives with only minor questions and perhaps a trivial revision. If management appears to have done its homework, the plans will nearly always be approved without serious question. Thus, the separation of management and ownership is accomplished.[10]

3. Once the objectives and plans have been "approved" the board maintains a hands-off relationship, but receives summary reports of the outcomes.

This three-step process may cause the board to appear to

be exercising genuine functions of direction, leading one to presume that they are more deeply involved in the goals of the firm than they are. Actually, the end effect of such a procedure is that the board can seldom innovate. Since they are executives in other firms or professionals in other lines, the directors may in fact see opportunities to improve objectives but are nevertheless constrained in their proposals. For example, they may have greater insight into ongoing social changes but are powerless to prevent the corporation from getting into serious trouble with its various publics. If the officers choose to ignore the less intangible objectives—which it must be added, many managements *do not* ignore—the effect is to sweep them under the rug. But in the long run, advocates such as Ralph Nader, the Sierra Club, the NAACP, or a legislative committee will rouse public opinion, which will in turn pressure legislators into passing laws which compel management to revise its objectives and change its behavior. The specific steps are executed by management and the costs of their implementation are borne by the company, but the outsiders get the credit. The board, meanwhile, plays its usual passive role.

The occupational safety and health act; standards for emissions from automobiles; truth in lending, packaging, and labeling; acts to clean up air and water—these are but a fraction of the areas offering opportunities for creative goal-setting by boards of directors that are almost never seen and acted upon.

The reasons why boards have seldom acted innovatively are understandable but unacceptable. They structure themselves and operate in such a way that they are constantly out of touch with reality. This remoteness from reality inclines them to setting faint goals. The strong conservatism of boards resides not only in the temperament of the members, but in their unwillingness to probe for facts which are needed for defining forward-looking goals.

47

Is it possible for boards to initiate change without intervening in administrative management? Yes, boards could if they were realistic about those issues which relate to goal-setting for the company. The directors are all members of society; they are knowledgeable in the ways of business; and they could insist upon getting the facts and participating strongly in goal-setting without engaging in crippling intervention in operations.

The most damning indictment of directors is that they are not only out of touch with reality in the operations of the firm but also in their major function, namely, performing strategic responsibilities.

THE LONE DIRECTOR'S KEY TO INFLUENCE

The route to swinging the laws onto the side of the stockholder and customer seem fairly lengthy and drawn out, and probably doomed to failure. One man in Virginia for years espoused the formation of a "stockholder's union" much like the labor unions to which workers belong. Proxy fights are expensive, doubtful of success, and require extensive organization. Yet the individual director who uses a few key questions in a determined and unremitting fashion can wield an extraordinary influence. This is especially true if the question is of the "What is our objective here?" type. It may be "What are we in business for?" or simply "Why?" or even "Why not?" If he is patient and asks the question only at crucial points, his weight will be felt and things will change. I once served as a member of a board and quietly asked, "Why aren't the financial statements presented to the board in conventional accounting presentation format?" (They looked like Benchley's treasurer's report.) The first time I was overwhelmed with a profusion of snow, to which I nodded understandingly in apparent acceptance. The next month I behaved as if my memory had completely failed me, and pretending I had never heard the answer, I repeated the same question. The reply was slightly confused and defensive. I nodded affably as if hearing it for the first time. After the third time that I repeated the question as if it were a wholly new idea, two things occurred. Other directors all turned their heads and listened most attentively to the reply. The next month the financial office was totally reorganized and reporting forms improved.

The key to good questioning that cannot arouse opposition is to be gentlemanly. If, of course, you are Norton Simon and own millions of shares, you can raise your voice and shout and raise a little hell, as he did with the management of Burlington Northern Railroad in 1973 when he stated that "boards of companies have gone dead." Norton used words such as "shape up" in jogging the board. This is perfectly fine when you are the largest stockholder (as Simon is at BN), but when you own a nominal number of shares, the soft but persistent *question* can move boards into assuming their leadership functions of defining strategies and objectives and reviewing management performance against them. Stockholders such as Wilma Soss who become strident are known as "gadflies." It is not that the redoubtable Mrs. Soss is not right; it is her style which creates a whole new defense. "She is objectionable in her manner, and therefore we can ignore her suggestions." This seems to be a flaw in her attack. The gentlemanly (or gentlewomanly) but persistent questioner who sticks to a few pertinent questions, rarely tweaks management's nose nor nips their heels on small matters, and never fails to find a chance to quietly prod the jugular vein can move things. Given a thousand such directors in strategic places, American industry could be reformed.

In following up on results against objectives, a retentive memory combined with some accurate notes helps also. Reflecting back with quiet accuracy on the campaign promises, perhaps given rashly under earlier questioning, is a punishing experience and assists management in learning to be responsible in making its rash commitments more closely attuned to the truth.

How Boards of Directors Miss Strategic Realities in Goal-setting

Directors recognize their limitations in making detailed operating judgments about the administration of the firm; hence, they end up as an almost uniformly conservative influence. The activity trap begins in the board room!

Directors are for the most part isolated from influence by the stockholders who elect them. The ownership of American corporations is concentrated in the hands of a minority. The top one percent of adult U.S. owners of wealth own 25 percent or more of all its personal and financial assets, reports Professor James D. Smith of Pennsylvania State University. Lewis Mandell of the University of Michigan states that 5 percent of all family units own 40 percent of all wealth, and the top 20 percent of the owners hold 80 percent of all assets. Upton and Lyons of the Cambridge Institute report even more drastic concentration in stock holdings in corporations: the richest one percent of stockholders own 62 percent of all publicly-held corporate stock, the richest 5 percent own 86 percent and the richest 20 percent own 97 percent (*Business Week*, August 5, 1972).

These large owners comprise a negligible force for change despite their potential influence, since they are likely to vote with management and to voice their dissatisfaction silently by selling their stock if the payoffs are inadequate. Here, too, the tendency is toward resistance to change rather than a general spirit of innovation.

The concentration of assets in trusts is an even greater deterrent to change. If the management continues to produce dividends and returns equivalent to alternative investments, a trustee is almost certain to vote his stock in favor of management proposals, including the election of directors proposed by management.

The end effect, then, is that management perpetuates itself, with the result that effective influences for change must come almost wholly from management itself or from its board of directors, and not from investors and owners.

The relationship of board members to the board itself is influenced by their relationship with the chairman. If he is not also the chief executive officer, chances are good that he is somewhat detached from the business. Only those managers who handle matters requiring direct board contact ordinarily go to such an officer for decisions.

The relationship of board members to senior officers of the firm, including the president, is likely to become increasingly passive. In any case, since these officers are themselves insulated from operations by layers of management, they usually lack knowledge sufficient to exploit strategic opportunities.

Few directors make their weight felt at board meetings. They traditionally engage in almost stereotyped forms of questioning and in careful use of calm and politic comment. In short, they display *low-intensity* behavior with respect to the company. This low intensity is exactly what the chairman, the president, and the officers of the firm want and expect, and it is what they ordinarily get.

The end effect of this top management situation is a built-in resistance to change at the top.

A president and an officer team that are innovative become essential if the company is to be made innovative. Because the directors have been chosen for their proven disinclination to make waves, it is a lucky accident that companies do nevertheless become innovative in so many instances. With low-intensity behavior a criterion for selection of board members, it would be surprising if the board chose teams of swingers for management positions. (Usually the reverse will be true: a hard-driving management team will use its influence to assure that a rubber-stamp board is chosen.) It is not really surprising that low-intensity boards should choose people most understandable to them, with predictably deadening effects upon the management behavior in the firm.

Clarence Randall, late president of Inland Steel, once observed that company presidents are lonely people.[11] They find they must isolate themselves from their organization, and in the process often isolate themselves from the truth. Eleven levels of management can produce a lot of filtering. It is small wonder that the top man, even in a small organization, is often deluded into acting upon "facts" that have been polished, trimmed, slanted, or even turned completely around. He is likely to make his contacts not downward but upward, with a conservative board, which situation leads to policies unsuitable for changing situations. Given such deprivation of valuable information, bloopers are common. Lots of youngsters, middle managers, and higher management then ask: "Do those people up there (that is, anybody two levels above) know what I want to do, what I can do, or even what I am doing now?"

The Fallacies in Board Decision-making

Isolated from the realities of the business, unwilling to make suggestions even in areas where directors have expertise, many boards fall into fallacious patterns. Without information and restrained by internal and external factors from obtaining it, they may reach decisions based on (1) preconceptions; (2) false polarization of issues; (3) overemphasis on compromise; (4) needless parallelism; (5) recourse to global but irrelevant issues; (6) conversion of hard facts into hypothetical questions; (7) authoritative but erroneous statements; (8) playing the role of devil's advocate; (9) tautological policies; or (10) assumptions that time alone will solve problems. An organization with a board prone to such errors lacks leadership—it has no head, merely a neck which grew up and haired over.

Since these ten major fallacies in board decision-making help to tighten the activity trap's grip on the entire organization (pockets of pointless activity can spring up anywhere of course), it may be worthwhile to look at each of them in more detail. The examples are factual but, except where the information is already public knowledge, the names of the companies have been omitted or disguised.

1. *Preconception instead of information.* People have biases —it is pointless to expect otherwise. Knowledgeable people can face this fact about themselves and take it into account in making their decisions. In the case of the modern board of directors, however, this normal bias is coupled with ignorance of reality and remoteness from the factual information that could remedy it. In these circumstances, preconceptions can easily take on heightened significance, and prejudice and bias, once established, become reinforced. The result is that information is received according to how well it fits the preconception. Evidence to the contrary is rejected as false, and the informant not only has his judgment questioned, but his reputation, if not his career, placed under a dark cloud of suspicion.

Take the case of the advertising agency board member whose preconception was that a certain supplier of direct mailing lists was the finest in the country. He touted this firm constantly. When confronted by the art director and copy chief with hard data proving that his lists were no longer producing business, he suggested possible bias and even blamed the post office. Though the entire direct mail division went deeply into the red, he persisted. As time passed, his preconception became known to management, and since he didn't hold any other important opinions, they were able to cope with his preconception.

Barred by custom from obtaining facts, directors will make decisions based on preconceptions. Ordinarily, a director may be permitted one bias without being considered guilty of unwarranted interference. Soft selling of his own products or that of his industry seems to be a common bias; a very few others may be allowed.

2. *False polarization.* This characterizes a decision-making system that divides every situation into black or white, X or Y, good guys or bad guys. "We must either go national in our sales campaigns or we go broke," declared one company president to his sales manager. Such a polarizing of options has a fatal flaw: not only does it ignore the middle ground, but it precludes other options which lie out in left field. This extreme logic discourages the search for the truly imaginative idea, for one of the options is usually unthinkable, thus leaving only its polar opposite for an action plan.

Take the case of a manufacturer of small electronic components whose Japanese competitors were outselling the company in the marketplace. The board was discussing alternatives. "Either we meet the Japanese competition head on and defeat it or we go broke," one director opined. His opinion held sway. But a few members of the market planning staff could think of alternatives that didn't include either of these possibilities. For example, they might buy the product from the Japanese manufacturer and sell it under their own label, as General Electric and some others were doing with television, or they might drop that line in favor of products that couldn't be beaten by Japanese competition. Yet these options and many others were never explored because the board made it clear that in its opinion only two options existed. Naturally, they couldn't come out in favor of going broke, so they were stuck with an untenable strategy. In the end the company did fail; thus the board had generated a self-fulfilling prophecy.

Such polarization of thinking was rampant in our country during the sixties. Either we continued fighting in Vietnam or all of Asia would fall like dominoes. Either we prosecuted dissenters or the country was doomed. Either the cigarette companies disproved Surgeon General Terry's report or they would go out of business. Of course, imaginative and open minds suggested other alternatives, and at least in the case of the tobacco companies, some of these were adopted. But not everyone listens. Boards without full information are often limited to one proposition or its diametric opposite.

3. *The contradiction compromise.* Some boards avoid facing reality by posing the problem as a contradiction to which there can be no satisfactory solution. This keeps things in dead center and obviates the necessity of changing anything. After all, if the "facts" show that to do nothing and to do something are equally dangerous, habit will keep the same old activities rolling. Furthermore, there is no possibility that the board will be charged with a mistake of commission.

The neon sign business of an outdoor display company was threatened by a new kind of plastic sign. "If we move ahead rapidly with the new sign, it may fail, and we will have thrown away our profits in neon signs. On the other hand, if we stick with neon and the new signs catch on, we will be caught short, and will probably fall behind." As a result of this succinct summary, no director would commit himself until the chairman jumped. He wouldn't decide, they didn't change, the new signs caught on, and the company fell into hard times.

4. *The needless parallelism snare.* Many boards find it reassuring to justify inaction and continuation of old activities by engaging in galloping parallelism. This is especially prevalent among the highly educated, it being practically epidemic on those boards where lawyers, economists, or other professionals

with high verbalizing skills are rampant. Take the personnel policy committee of one board which was responsible for straightening out a troublesome problem in union relations. This committee soberly stated: "With the workers and supervisors thinking and feeling on several levels at the same time, the morale and production implications of programs and procedures have short run and lasting causes and effects." They really said that.

Look at the parallels. The workers and the supervisors. They think and they feel. Do the supervisors think and the workers feel, or vice versa? Or does each group do both? Are the morale implications the same as the production implications? They certainly are not, and nobody has really proved a cause-and-effect relationship between them. Do the programs suffer from the morale of the supervisors? the productivity of the workers? Do the procedures suffer from the feeling of workers? One could produce about 100 combinations from these matched parallels. Meanwhile, nothing new was appearing to solve the problem.

One professor of my acquaintance has a large rubber stamp in his desk which he uses to grade student papers. When he sees nonsense such as the above, he boldly stamps BULLSHIT across the face of the paper. Presumably nobody does this for boards of directors, no matter how badly it is needed. Everyone just keeps on behaving the same old way at board meetings.

5. *The global issue swamp.* Some boards turn the most simple proposal into a metaphysical question of deeply intellectual character.

A bright young executive from a consulting firm was hired with an interesting proposition by a large midwestern company. He could work at turning around a sick group of divisions as a senior vice-president for one year, whereupon he could remain with that group or become an executive vice-president. At the end of the year, the chairman was instructed to ask him whether or not he wished to transfer. Two board members promptly turned it into a metaphysical issue. "The entire policy of self-determination and career guidance is at stake here. I think we should seriously consider the larger issue. Total career management programs for the company should be fully explored before we make a specific decision in this narrow instance." After two months of inaction on his transfer, the young executive resigned to join a Chicago company which offered him the presidency in six months. The original company never did get an answer to the larger question, and they lost a good man.

6. *Converting facts into hypothetical questions.* An oft-employed fallacy which snaps the activity trap shut around a board is that of turning a real question of fact into a hypothetical case study and then treating the hypothetical case as though it were the real one.

One food producer was scooped by a competitor's research breakthrough which enabled the competitor to capture a lucrative market in a single quarter. Rather than asking "What do we do to catch up?" the board preferred to grapple with the hypothetical issue: "If we had redirected our research into basic food chemistry rather than minor packaging research, what would the effect have been?" For the next three months the research-production committee spent two hours each week reconstructing a fictional case of what might have happened if they had reallocated their budget along different lines in the past year. By the time they had explained the error completely to themselves, the new product had captured the market and was unassailable.

Recently at the board meeting of an electronics company, a director outlined the mistake the Chrysler Corporation had made in 1954 in borrowing 100 million dollars from the Prudential Insurance Company, demonstrating clearly to his audience how superior equity financing would have been for the company by 1971. But he never stated just how all this related to the electronics firm. Similar fictional reconstruction was used by a board member who pointed out how the steel industry would have benefited from Japanese methods of adopting new technology as fast as it emerged. His analysis, which was given in 1970, covered the period 1946 to 1960. As escape from reality it was superb, but of course it was irrelevant to the situation at hand.

The difficulty lies both in not facing the situation as it exists in the present and in failing to come up with forward-looking rather than backward-looking prescriptions. Some directors prefer to describe the past situation, rather than face the present, point out a direction, and order "March!"

7. *The erroneous authoritative statement.* A frequently overlooked but nevertheless overriding factor in corporate life is that once boards issue declarative statements, these statements are accepted as gospel by the company, and the machinery of power moves people in the direction indicated. This is fine if the directives make the *right things* happen, but woe to the company if the board is wrong! Should the board state: "The fault lies with the selling techniques we are using," then the sales techniques are apt to change in some way, even though the fault may lie elsewhere—with product strategy, pricing, product mix, or weak advertising. Power is heady stuff which, unlike sex, alcohol, or other physical-need fulfillers, has no apparent point of diminishing return. The exercise of power becomes an end in itself. Declarative statements from the top of the company resound down through the plant, the sales department, the engineering department, and produce a flurry of execution. The big wheels make a quarter turn and the little wheels make thirty-two revolutions. Even a low-intensity board may, in an occasional spasm of power-play, purge any opposition to itself. Disagreement quickly takes on connotations of disloyalty, bad judgment, unsoundness, or at least abrasiveness. The board that can't obtain access to facts but learns to relish its own power is even more dangerous than a passive one.

8. *The role of devil's advocate*. Many a board sees its major role as that of critic and judge of proposals. When an officer proposes something new, such a board or one of its members adopts the role of demolition expert with great relish. "I tear into every proposal to help the man find holes in it. If I can puncture his ideas, you can bet that he hasn't thought it through and he leaves with his tail between his legs." And, we might add, seldom comes back with another new idea.

A subordinate says of the board: "They seem to enjoy tearing into ideas coming from below. In some cases they do catch a flaw, but in most cases they are like a district attorney badgering a witness. Nobody likes to get chopped up for thinking of something good. If Mr. —— would only express some appreciation for my *having* an idea, then be a little more gentle in the way he finds the flaws, I might feel better about trying to help the company with some money-making ideas. I have a desk drawer full of ideas I think would save us money, but I'm damned if I will crawl on my belly over cracked glass trying to sell him something which he should be eager to hear."

One board member states: "My greatest contribution is screening ideas. My greatest problem is that so few of our managers *have* any."

For most managers who work for such a board, it is the same old thing: activity as usual, and try to have this board or its troublesome members replaced with some less intense types.

9. *Something equals itself*. In the field of logic, tautology denotes a statement demonstrating that something equals itself. Most boards tend strongly to tautology.

One board found two officers, the controller and sales manager, at odds. Yet the board refused to deal with the issues between the two. "Salesmen are hired to sell, and controllers to control," was their sober opinion. While that is an indisputable statement, it is not only a tautology but a harmful partial truth in this case. Tautology, because it is so obviously true, may obscure the fact that it is only a *half* truth. By point-

59

ing out that something equals itself, the statement seems to take on the character of Truth Discovered, and all who question it may appear of suspect mental qualities, if not inferior moral character. So they stop arguing and resume the same old activity that consumes resources with less and less output.

10. *Time-will-tell delusion.* When confronted with hard evidence that the company is on a collision course with disaster, some boards raise their sights and declare that, although such an outcome may seem apparent in the short run, things will work out better in the long run if the present course is followed. "If we see the whole situation from the overall viewpoint and continue to watch carefully until we have all of the information in hand, of course we'll see that in the big picture it's better to keep going as before."

Sometimes, it is true, the higher levels *do* have information not available to lesser ranks and sometimes, too, persistence *is* the right answer. The danger here comes from the isolation of top from middle and lower ranks which permits the board to rely upon an argument, valid or otherwise, that cannot be disputed by those who don't occupy such lofty status.

Time itself is often vested with curative and therapeutic powers by some executives. "Give it time, and time is on our side." Time, of course, doesn't do anything by itself; it merely provides a framework in which affirmative actions can take place or in which something can be killed.

The Need for Reasonable Adventurers as Directors

Stanley Vance has studied boards of directors extensively and concluded that they are generally in unsatisfactory positions to contribute all they might and that restructuring them so that they offer the optimum credentials background and focus of interest would increase their effectiveness. Other scholars generally agree that in General Motors, General Electric, Dupont, and other leading corporations there has been a firm expectation to get maximum usefulness from the board, with plans for enforcement.

Structure and procedure alone, however, won't cure the problems when boards of directors don't direct, are out of touch with reality, and, when they function, do so in a stultifyingly conservative, anti-innovative manner. The situation demands that the board behave as a group of *reasonable adventurers*. The term is adopted from a study done over a period of ten years of Princeton undergraduates by Roy Heath, who found it possible to place students into categories along a continuum, with the adventurer (the plunger, the crapshooter) at one end and the man who is so obsessed with reason that he *never* commits himself at the other. Since the study relates to college graduates, it isn't directly applicable to selection and guidance of directors. However, Heath's model of the reasonable adventurer has much to commend it. He is rational, insists upon sufficient facts to make decisions, and uses logic to grasp reality and comprehend his situation. At the same time he is venturesome enough to move steadily toward improvement and to make reality-based commitments entailing risks, which he attempts to minimize by thorough study and logical calculations of the probabilities of success.[12]

A board composed of such men could direct the corporation without intervening in the proper functions of officers and managers.

1. *They would conserve* the assets entrusted to them and retain the best features of present practices.

2. *They would introduce change* in an orderly, rational, and conscious fashion in establishing and modifying objectives that require such change, by unleashing the creative powers already in existence in the organization and by rewarding such creativity and innovation when it appears.

3. *They would be an example* of how managers and lower

61

rank employees should comport themselves. As teachers of reasonable adventuring for the corporation, they would be developers of an ongoing supply of men and women like themselves.

How to Build and Maintain an Ideal Board

Opportunities to overhaul and renew boards don't occur every month, but there are some moves that can be readied and made available for use when the time comes. There are other actions by present boards to upgrade themselves which can occur more immediately. Of course, there are a few situations where nothing can be done short of a few well-placed retirements or funerals. Patience is necessary even if not an unalloyed virtue.

1. The present board can choose a president who understands how to get maximum value from a board. To some, this will seem to be a call for a puppet or a flunky, which of course is not desirable. Yet, the president or chief executive who understands strategic goal-setting and the management of the board and its committees will go a long way toward giving emphasis to the best behavior of boards. When the time comes to pick a president, a searching look at his understanding of how to maximize board contribution should be added to the selection criteria.

2. The present board can await a crisis and use the incident to produce a therapeutic switch in the behavior and attitude of the management. The Chrysler board in 1960 provides a model for such a takeover. Changes such as those in J. I. Case following the profit crunch under Mr. Graede in the fifties or when TWA went through upheavals which produced the exit of Howard Hughes are further examples of crises which afford opportunities to remake the face of the corporation.

3. A single bad year, a drop in profits, the decline of market

share, or similar serious but not fatal crises afford many opportunities for the board to speak with heightened emphasis. Not as serious as the earthquake level upheaval in earlier paragraphs, it provides enough of a humility-inducing climate that those who wish to make quiet improvements will find the time propitious.

The common ingredient in all of these reform efforts lies in the board winning over the presidency and chief executive position to one of greater responsiveness. This germinal position, once won, will have extraordinary influence upon the rest of management, for the powers of the presidency are ordinarily fairly authoritative. The idea is not to crumble the man in order to remake him closer to the board's wishes, but to educate him.

The major vehicle for reforming boards, making them more effective, lies in teaching the president to be a skilled listener. The board then can rely upon orderly, rational, and conscious attention to goals, resulting ultimately in turning the company in its entirety toward being goals- and results-, rather than activity-centered.

Chapter 4

The End of Motivation

The activity trap kills motivation.

DESTROYING OR OBSCURING PEOPLE'S GOALS is the surest way of killing motivation. By centralizing management and extending only limited trust to lower levels, the company stifles any goal-setting on a widespread basis. Yet lip service is rendered to the need to *motivate* employees, salesmen, engineers, managers, and executives. If managers could explain why people behave the way they do, somebody might go a step further and motivate that behavior for the benefit of the company.

The customary pattern for applying motivational theory (i.e., explanation of motives) is to examine the *individual* and catalog his needs, desires, aspirations, interests, drives, and the like. After these have been laid out for inspection and then rearranged in cause-and-effect relationships, controls can be worked out, such as pay systems, employee benefits, or human relations practices by management. Such analysis, however, seems to neglect the utmost importance of *the goal itself as a motivational influence*—perhaps not complete in itself but certainly primary in timing and importance.

A THREE-FACTOR THEORY OF MOTIVATION

A *motive* is "an inner state that energizes, activates, or moves (hence motivation), and that directs or channels behavior toward goals," according to one widely accepted definition.[1] The attention of most researchers and observers of motivation focuses almost exclusively on the inner states of the person, ignoring the vital role that the goal itself plays in motivation. The goal is in fact the first of three major factors in motivation; internal drives are the second, with payoff systems the third. It is not practical to explicate all the facets of each (there is a plethora of literature), but their relationship and priorities can be briefly stated.

GOALS AS THE FIRST FACTOR IN MOTIVATION

Objectives are hoped-for outputs of behavior; they are the conditions which will exist if the efforts of the person or organization are successful. John K. Galbraith suggests that the problem of goals arises with the relation of the individual to the organization. The individual must know what his own personal goals are and what the organization expects of him. The corporation which defines its goals but systematically fails to make clear how the individual can, by helping in the pursuit of those goals, move toward attainment of his own objectives, kills motivation as surely as the denial of food and water denies life. A common misconception is that it is unnecessary to define goals for employees—that merely to prescribe *activity* is sufficient. The misconception, if acted upon, has chilling, deadly effects. How this misconception arises is known: it is a result of logical fallacies.

Seeing workers through preconceived images and not individually is a form of fallacy. Management treats the "work

65

force" as an aggregate, with no provision for individual differences. The fallacy lies in regarding the image as the *only* reality. Yet the practice of attributing weak or immoral habits to an entire body, as though it were an individual, is of long standing in management as well as in the populace. To picture labor as a cunning beast, to think in such terms as "the scientific mind," "the legal mind," "the engineering mind," or "the staff mentality," produces policies which make such images self-fulfilling prophecies. People are regarded as animals, and the simplistic operant conditioning that disciples of B. F. Skinner have applied to the training of pigeons or sea lions is extrapolated to humans. The master of one prep school is reported to have viewed the boys there like beagle dogs—forever running and panting with mouths open and tails wagging—and governed his institution accordingly. Lots of running in open fields, keeping them well fed, interspersed by training with generous use of the willow switch comprised the managerial policies of his organization.

The end result of stereotyping employees rather than arranging for individual identification with company goals produces activity-centered people.

The mechanistic approach has an even more depressing effect on motivation than a zoomorphic one. Here, workers are perceived as "instrumental" men like machines or other inanimate objects. What distinguishes this mechanistic conception from the previous one, in which the mass of employees are treated as animals, is that numbers, machines, or instruments are even more dehumanized. A donkey has a will, but an automaton does not. Simply find the mechanical linkages, provide an energizing motor, push the right buttons, and the machine will run smoothly unless, of course, there is a mechanical fault, in which case a mechanic is needed. The manager is the machine-designer and perhaps its tender; the staff

66

is the lubrication crew. The policies which emerge from such a conception of the work force are mechanical and activity-centered, for it is unthinkable that the gear or the drive belt should have objectives which are distinct from the purposes of the machine.[2]

Similarly, to think of employees as possessing a single quality is fallacious and deleterious image-making. Many a company town has been organized on the basis of some narrow image of employees. The paternalistic owner viewed the employees as children of a very large familial group, with time for work, play, church, hobbies, and the like. This image made his role and theirs clear, and often produced from the employees exactly the kind of dependent behavior found in children in large families.

The *one-dimensional man*, another variant of image-making about employees, lies behind many managerial motivational practices. Such thinking has produced a theory of economics in which life is nasty, brutish, and short, because one-dimensional men, according to the theory, are doomed to live at subsistence levels by their fatal tendency to procreate, which creates an oversupply of labor that consumes more than can be produced. In managing managers, some executives view all subordinates —Thomas Hobbes created the phrase in *The Leviathan*—as having a "restless and perpetual desire after power which ceaseth only after death."[3] Shaping goals collaboratively with such men is considered folly because it appears to weaken the possibilities of retaining power in the leader. The advertising business still operates in such a fashion, with elaborate political systems to make sure that no account executive acquires such control of his accounts that he might use it to grasp the entire agency. Frequent firing is a characteristic of such organizations. The fallacy of "the economic man" is still pervasive; it assumes that employees work for money and promotions to the exclusion of everything else.

Each of these images tends to act like a self-fulfilling prophecy. The man who finds that the only rewards in his work are economic will adapt himself to the situation, thus proving to the boss that he is indeed an economic man. The same thing is true of the false image of man as *the consistent man*, people being regarded as universally alike. This assumption produces policies that take consistency for granted. Of course, one does find consistencies in men, just as one finds that they are indeed *sometimes* economically oriented or child-like or animallike. But to adopt a simplistic image rather than a more complex one leads to policies which foster precisely that kind of behavior. The fallacy of *mass man* is often found in the marketing policies of companies, especially in scheduling and programming of television shows. The image of the customer as a boob sitting around in his T-shirt ripping the tops off beer cans while he stares at his video tube has the self-fulfilling effect of producing a substantial number of programs that are beamed directly at him—and of finding him there. Herbert Marcuse in *One Dimensional Man* asks why, if individuals are satisfied to the point of happiness with things handed down to them by their managers, should they insist upon change? An even more radical suggestion by Marcuse is: If individuals are preconditioned to receive satisfying thoughts, feelings, and aspirations, why should they want to make waves and think, feel, and aspire for themselves?[4]

Image-thinking that is simplistic in scope produces men who will adapt to the image. When these images all have the effect of reinforcing activity and of making personal goal-setting productive of unfavorable consequences, activity becomes an end in itself.

The personnel processes of selection, promotion, compensation, performance appraisal, critical notes inserted into personnel folders, training courses, coaching by the boss of employees in the intraoffice version of the marital "pillow talk" —these are all designed to produce activity-centered people.

Job descriptions, written standards against which people are hired and trained, are statements about activity rather than goals and output. They comprise an immense reinforcer of the activity trap. The training course for most supervisors is riddled with instructions as to style, including the ways to think, talk, write, and relate. The appraisal system produces periodic written records which are filed, testifying in the words of a colleague-judge who is present on a daily basis about how well the subordinate has nestled himself into the confines of the activity trap. Words such as *diligent, intelligent, loyal,* and *efficient* are rewarding words for complying with prescribed activity. Words such as *hostile, noncooperative, defiant,* and *insubordinate* are reserved for people who fly in the face of prescribed activities.[5] If the hostile and defiant employee happens to be more productive for both the organization and himself, that productivity can easily be overlooked in the activity trap.

Motivation is not necessarily equated with productivity, unless management defines objectives for the organization. Given a board of directors who do not define goals, the responsibility for goal-definition falls to the full-time management of the firm. Since it creates the one-dimensional images, management itself produces the activity trap, which the owners and the board of directors, by abdication, permit and endorse. In higher management, the forces militating against individual goal-setting and independent action for their attainment include the desire of those in higher management to retain their present positions until retirement, and also their need to be surrounded by reliable people who will respect that wish and support it in order to be able to enjoy successor status.

The end result is an oligarchy (aided by key committees who define the real objectives of the firm) plus some special-

69

ized subordinate groups such as scientists, accountants, manufacturing men, sales experts, and lawyers who are masters of the families of activities that comprise their professions. The motivational gap arises when the individual finds that his personal objectives are dropping out of sight—that he cannot attain them within his cluster of activities. When people are fortunate enough to work for an organization that has goals defined in such painstaking detail that the individual can hitch his own personal goals to them, the unleashed energy and ingenuity make that organization great. The findings of behavioral scientists such as David McClelland, Fred Herzberg, Abraham Maslow, and Rensis Likert suggest a connection between goal-setting and motivation that is just beginning to be utilized by a few leaders in organization and management. In brief, these are some of their conclusions:

1. Motivation properly starts with anticipatory goal states.

2. Motivation is a possession of responsible individuals who are committed to attainment of these anticipatory future states.

3. Only a very few motives are innate or natural, and they are mainly physiological (hunger, sex, and the like) rather than emotional.

4. The overwhelming body of motivation is learned, secondary, social, or psychogenic, and almost all such motives are goal-directed. McClelland suggests that every motive involves two states: "a present state which redisintegrates through past learning a second state."[6]

An objective is a potent motivator. When objectives are systematically denied, or when activity is substituted for goals, motivation declines.

5. Motivation has no single cause. It changes as the more important goals are attained, it is affected by both conscious and unconscious influences, and it evolves throughout a per-

70

son's life. The best insight into normal motivation comes through observation of normal persons, not of rats, cats, primates, and abnormal persons.[7]

6. Motivation improves if due attention is paid to the objective-setting process, the defining of corporate and divisional goals, the methods of stating managerial and employee objectives, and the procedural problems of goal-setting.

The Removal of Obstacles to Achievement

Clear goals (in contrast to meaningless activity) *energize* the organism. They support not only persistent activity but variable activity. When President Kennedy proposed a goal of putting a man on the moon by 1970, he released a veritable flood of activity of immensely varied nature, much of which was totally unpredictable in its character and complexity. The *goal as a motivating condition* directs the individual and produces planning, organizing, controlling, and other conventional management processes. In truth, many goal-centered behaviors are ineffective, but skills in managing individuals can be studied, practiced, acquired, and improved. However, this learning and directing of behavior must follow the goal-setting because the goal serves as a *discriminatory criterion* for choosing among alternative courses of action. Moreover, it is a guide to decision-making and a basis for review and feedback that will control, halt, defer, redirect, and change behavior. The goal also serves as a yardstick for judging outside influences for selective choices.

Administratively, however, more is required of the motivational process than mere goal-setting. *In large organizations, management must accept responsibility for removing the obstacles to goal-attainment.* This can be illustrated by a simple example:

A party of hikers lost near the Grand Canyon saw an old prospector with his burro. They asked him how to get to the

71

nearest town. "Wal," he suggested, "you could go three miles straight across the canyon if you was a crow, or 55 miles around it."

Simply pointing out a goal and even defining some general paths is not sufficient management behavior to produce motivational effects. Pointing out a cafeteria to a hungry man is worthless if the door to the cafeteria is locked. Setting goals which are removed from possible attainment by insuperable walls is pointless, frustrating, and cruel, but that is exactly what many managers practice: "I demand results, not excuses."

A large public utility was concerned because its engineers did not get their reports written on time. Management railed at the engineers' lack of motivation and dedication, and ruminated about possible punishments for those who persisted in their failure. But an engineer's story put the matter in a different light.

"We all work out on the floor in one large room, and the noise and distraction are deadly for continued thought. Even when you get it done at home, you can't get it typed in the typing pool because engineering reports get the lowest priorities and the typists with lowest skill levels are assigned to them. Then when you get it finished, the sales department will reject it and you have to start all over because it was in the wrong style, yet they won't put out a style manual we can follow."

The interference which is built into the job conditions frequently prevents the employee from attaining his goal. In some instances the information which is received either is wrong or is designed to prevent freedom of effort.

A simple method of determining whether or not the stated goals could be attained by normal people has been devised by Dr. Geary Rummler, head of a New York consulting firm. Called a "consequence grid," it looks something like the following:

72

THE CONSEQUENCE GRID

		Behavior of the Individual	
		Productive of goals desired	Unproductive of goals desired
Consequences to the person	Favorable	I	III
	Unfavorable	II	IV

The four blank spaces are filled in with the consequences to the person for behaving in each of the two classes of behavior. In the upper left-hand square I are listed major favorable consequences to the person for behaving in a productive fashion, and under II are listed unfavorable consequences to him for doing the right things. Then the same procedure is repeated for III and IV, listing consequences for unproductive behavior.

If the favorable consequences to the person for doing the right things are small, and the favorable consequences for doing the wrong things are high, and the unfavorable consequences for doing right outweigh the favorable consequences for doing wrong, you can count on wrong things happening. This is also true if there is little difference between outcomes.

The second requirement in a motivational system is the removal of obstacles. Such obstacles need attention from above when they prevent people from going toward goals which they understand clearly and are committed to attaining. They may be blocked by managerial policy or lack of facilities and assistance. Rensis Likert has labeled the cluster of corrective managerial behaviors "supportive management," and his research shows that it is present in the best-run organizations.[8]

Supportive management is in large part the removal of obstacles that are very real to the subordinate but are perhaps unknown and unseen by the manager who causes them to be erected. The engineering manager above was unable to see the distractions his engineers suffered in the large room and their difficulties in working through a nonsupportive typing pool. When the manager did see the obstacles, he was able to arrange different facilities and procedures which removed them: the construction of some cubicles to which engineers might retire to write free from distraction, the assignment of typists directly to the engineering department, and the preparation of a standard style manual for reports were the "motivational" forces which allowed the committed engineer to attain his objectives.

This obstacle-easing is a step beyond the Pavlovian stimulus-response theory of behavior, for it is not the stimulus of a private room and a competent secretary that triggered the reports to be written but the commitment of responsible people to the completion of an agreed-upon objective. The example illustrates how the environment, which can serve as a prod and a whip to useful behavior, can in many instances squelch and prevent it.[9]

Escape and avoidance comprise far too much of the behavior of middle and upper managers, but this is far more universal. The hostile, opposing, and contradictory forces which seem to surround the world of work are well recognized in numerous half-jesting but quickly recognized "laws"—"anything that can go wrong will do so" and "things left alone get worse." Adverse conditions permitted to accumulate in the work environment can stop the best-intentioned person. The function of supportive management is to discover and eradicate obstacles in the path of subordinates by permitting free expressions of opinion defining obstacles and allowing wide latitude for obstacle-removing behavior in lower ranks. More

74

is required than just exhorting managers to stop acting like tyrants; they must be trained to a positive responsibility for finding and demolishing the barriers to subordinates' achievement.

When excessive report-writing cuts into the creative function of teaching children, schoolteachers are in need of supportive management which simplifies the reporting system. Salesmen whose time is squandered in pointless meetings, fruitless activity reports, and profitless responses to trivial inquiries rather than in meeting customer needs could use a more supportive style of management to eradicate these systematic obstacles.

The brilliant preacher and biblical scholar who is enmeshed in clerical and custodial work needs a board which will see that these obstacles to his highest level of contribution are removed from his path.

J. K. Galbraith in *The New Industrial State* proposes a general theory of motivation which prescribes four major categories of motivational explanation. (1) The individual goes toward the group goals by *compulsion*. (2) The acceptance of the group's goal is purchased; this Galbraith calls *pecuniary* motivation. (3) The individual may be so taken with the goals of some group that he suspends his previous personal goals and adopts those of the group as his own; in other words, he *identifies*. (4) The final class is for the individual who sees in the group's goals a vehicle for attaining his own personal goals or a possibility of affecting the goals of the group to conform with his personal goals; this Galbraith calls *adaptive* motivation.[10]

Organizations in which activity has become the primary basis of classification of goals tend to adopt the compulsory or pecuniary forms of motivation. More activity is considered better than less, even activity which has been robbed of meaning. The supportive style of management, which is primarily an obstacle-removal approach, permits and encourages the identification and adaptive modes of motivation to come into play.

Motivation by Payoffs

The third requirement for a sound motivational system is the striking of a balance between person and organization. "You keep paying me and I will keep laying these bricks." The wall these bricks comprise may serve no useful purpose, but the willingness of the worker to proceed anyway is a consequence of emphasizing payoffs rather than identity of personal goals with organizational goals or the possibility that the work will affect the organization's goals. Payoffs are part of a system that Herzberg has called KITA, which can be impolitely summed as "kick in the anatomy" motivation, a highly refined art in many management circles.[11] It is sufficiently refined for Herzberg to classify KITA influences as *positive* (a form of reward such as Galbraith would include in his pecuniary motivation) and *negative* (roughly Galbraith's compulsion motivation). Herzberg includes among payoffs those rewards that are forthcoming when the company offers fair pay, generous benefit plan, and good working conditions. These have no positive motivational effects, but their absence can serve as a *"demotivator."* They serve as a kind of organizational hygiene. The individual psychologically discounts the motivational effects of things that every employee receives in his own company and in most other companies.

The true motivators in the payoff area, Herzberg suggests, are those which are not included in the KITA forms of motivation. They are in the intangible satisfactions of self-expression and self-actualization which come from high levels of attainment. Abraham Maslow has likewise classified motivating influences in hierarchies, with physical satisfactions occupying the lowest level. The highest levels of motivation, Maslow ex-

76

plains, are those which have to do with the creative, the self-actualization and self-expression experiences. Both Herzberg's and Maslow's motivators correspond to Galbraith's identification and adaptive motivators.

All of the higher levels of motivational influences require the presence of objectives, to which the individual can commit himself and for which he can feel some personal responsibility. Without these prior conditions, no motivational effects are possible except through pecuniary means, KITA, and compulsion.

The activity-centered organization is barren of the highest and best levels of motivation and must rely on compulsion and pecuniary or other physical rewards at perhaps a constantly increasing rate to maintain what becomes meaningless work.

When empirical evidence reveals that large numbers of people are accommodating themselves to pecuniary rewards or submitting passively to a compulsion to work for its own sake, we find people who have disappeared into their job descriptions.

Once I visited a large factory where row on row of workers were inserting large sheets of metal into a press, which descended with a crash to form metal shells, one a minute, all day long.

"Doesn't it make you sad to see men doing that for a living?" I asked the personnel manager. He smiled.

"Oh, they *like* it!"

"That makes me even sadder," I said.

Chapter 5

Why Most Problems
Don't Get Solved and
Many Get Worse

In activity-centered organizations most problems don't get solved and many get worse.

PICTURE A TYPICAL MANAGERIAL PROBLEM-SOLVING CONFERENCE. The boss, or the convener of the conference, calls everyone to order and opens the meeting with some prefatory remarks, along the lines of, "Well, I guess you know we are here to talk about the Frammis contract." Everybody nods glumly. Somebody might then suggest that they review the facts. Each one contributes his findings, if any, and corrects and modifies the evidence of others until the group generally agrees that they have the facts or have at least labeled the ones they need. Then comes the next stage. Somebody tries to summarize what the problem is. The group all contributes, and it sounds something like what follows:

"Well, I think the problem is clearly one of ———"

"Is that really the problem? Doesn't your problem really produce another which is more serious?"

This process of pushing the problem up and down a chain of cause and effect occurs endlessly. Try it yourself, in the interest of learning. The next time somebody tells you he has a problem, ask him to name it.

When he has named the problem, then ask him, "Is that really the problem?" He will immediately change the problem to something else. Keep asking the question and he will keep switching the problem.

What's happening here? In part, it happens because we haven't a system for attacking problem-solving. Unfortunate consequences follow, all of which reinforce the activity trap. We hang on to a problem because we can't define it. There are some other reasons we don't solve problems but, for the time being, let's see what happens when we get stuck in the initial stages.

At first, the problem is an *irritant* and we swat at it.

If it is large enough, it becomes a *terror*—it sets our adrenalin flowing, and we show rage or terror.

After several attempts at a solution, we are most likely to find *fragmentary solutions*. This seems to be a common practice, what Herbert Simon has called "satisficing" the problem. We find a solution which is "satisfactory-sufficient" (hence the new word).[1]

If we can solve many or most of our problems temporarily, we *develop toleration* of the rest. This could be described as a *narcotic* effect. We give ourselves temporary ease from the pain of the problem.[2] Our daughter married a bum? Our sales manager ran off and started his own firm with our largest account? Three of our top engineers resigned at a crucial point in the development project? After the initial shock, our narcotizing facility takes over.

In retrospect, our problems take on a more glamorous and romantic air; they become glorious things, prized possessions about which we boast *because of* their magnitude, immensity, difficulty, and insolubility.

After some extended experience in living through this sequence

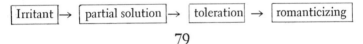

Irritant → partial solution → toleration → romanticizing

79

the tendency to keep cool in the face of problems is more prevalent. This means that the activity trap takes over, for we have lost the edge that could have impelled us to find solutions.

The Atlantic Ocean off the coast of northern New England is paralyzingly cold much of the year. Even on the hottest day in summer, the water temperature is at a level that shocks the innocent, first-time bather and sends him reeling back to the beach. Yet the natives, especially the small children, romp in and out of the surf, splashing the cryogenic stuff on themselves without apparently noticing that it is barely above the block-ice level. After some long and tortuous testing and self-punishment, even the summer visitor becomes accustomed to the water, and by the end of his vacation wonders why the casual visitor seems so affected by it upon first contact. This ability of people to accommodate extends to more than the Atlantic Ocean; it extends also to the development of toleration of what should be intolerable conditions at work, in the home, in government. Unless we can keep people's toleration level low enough for the important problems, they will not be solved.

This highly developed toleration for problems which should be intolerable is a major element in reinforcing the activity trap.

WHAT IS A PROBLEM?

The most likely way of solving a problem is to get it into the hands of a responsible party (not responsible for causing it, but for *solving* it), obtain a commitment that he will accept responsibility for its solution, define the conditions that will exist when the problem is solved, and then step aside, except to help as needed.

The definition of the problem then becomes "achieving the objective agreed upon." A problem thus becomes a deviation from some objective. If we know where we are, and wish to be

80

elsewhere, then the dimension of the problem is the distance between here and there. This definition, proposed by Professor Simon, has some marvelous advantages in facilitating problem-solving.

It turns the vague and general into a concrete goal for attainment.

It defines the limits of the problem. We start where we are, and define solutions as attaining some different position.

It converts the problem into an objective for some responsible person or group.

Weyerhauser Timber Company provides a happy example of how this approach was applied by management to its safety problem during the sixties. Doing business in an industry which is traditionally hazardous to life and limb, the officers of the giant firm were determined to make work safe in their forests and mills. Traditional timbering and mills alibis which identified the problem in circular fashion were set aside and, starting with a specific definition of where they were, management converted this information into an indicator or two which would be the rallying point for everyone. The "frequency rate" became the center of attention (man-hours multiplied by a million divided by the number of lost time accidents). The indicator was dramatized, with top management stating its objective of reducing it and making it emphatic to all hands. Engineering changes, personnel policies, production rules, and motivational programs followed. The result was a decline of some 80 percent in lost time accidents. Safety became an IOU, which each employee owed everyone else: workers, boss, peers. By 1973 Vice-President Harry Morgan was able to report to the Forest Produce Industry Conference that work was safer at Weyerhauser than in most other lines of activity in which employees functioned, including their homes, their cars, or on vacation.

Thus, the game described at the start of this chapter is averted. Rather than leaping from problem to problem, and

81

sliding back and forth between causes and effects, our attention is focused on specific factual matters:

Where are we now?

Where would we like to be? By what period of time?

Who is to accept responsibility for getting us there?

The Difficult Search for Causation

With such a problem definition in hand, we return again to the task of examining a storehouse of data and salvaging from it a few valuable artifacts of *cause*. (Not *who*, but *what* caused it?) Indeed, if we can find the causes of the problem which we have defined so boldly, we might be able to eliminate and return things to normal, attaining the objective sought. The definition of such a course is easier than its execution. Suppose that a manual for automobile owners to use in repairing their vehicles included just two steps:

How to Repair Your Car

1. Find the trouble.
2. Fix it!

This would hardly be considered a satisfactory guide, however correct it might be. There are some major barriers to finding causes which may be worth noting; they are common fallacies and, accordingly, keep us from solving problems.[3]

The Tendency to Scapegoat

In large organizations and small, the scapegoat method of solving problems is widespread. Like the one above, it has two parts:

How to Fix a Business Problem

1. Find the stupid guy who caused it.
2. Fire him!

Such practices are more prevalent in some places than others. There is no doubt that the two-step process outlined above is widely employed. The consequences to the man fired are, of course, unsatisfactory because he is unemployed. The consequences to the organization may be worse because everyone else is now less inclined to take chances. Simply stick to the old activity, to the things you have always done; don't vary them unless somebody expressly gives you orders. And even then, it's smart to get it in writing, which makes somebody higher up, and not you, responsible. The result? A steady decline in innovation—the activity trap wins again.

By *scapegoating* the problem rather than finding the causes, only one symptom has been treated and the opportunity of finding a basic cause and averting repetition has been lost. The search for causes has often become a posse seeking an unlucky suspect, and the whole subject of search for causation has accordingly fallen into disrepute. It evokes images of congressional committee hearings which drag a series of people into the limelight for the political advantage of the committee chairman.

THE IMMOBILIZED ORGANIZATION

The search for causes of problems is necessarily backward-looking since past events must be examined. Some of them are labeled "causes" and the others "effects." Overemphasis on finding causation for every problem does little good; indeed it can immobilize the organization eventually. If everyone spends his time looking for causes of every untoward event, nothing new will be done. The activity trap is made more viable and its clutches are strengthened.

The only practical justification for finding causes is to solve a problem or to assure a better future. When the search for causes reverts to picking over the rubbish heap of past events for scandals and scapegoats, it is unworthy and unproductive work.[4]

83

The reason most administrators and executives look for causes today seems to be to find opportunities for improvement. The idea expressed by some anonymous speaker that "a problem is an opportunity in disguise" is relevant here. Given the overall assumption that managers are going to use causal explanations for good reasons (to find opportunities) and will heroically avoid lapsing into bad reasons (to seek scapegoats), there still are a lot of fallacies into which they can slip in relating cause and effect. At least nine major pitfalls appear worthy of identifying and describing:

1. The chicken-egg fallacy.
2. Mixing causation and association.
3. Putting the effect before the cause.
4. The oversimplification fallacy.
5. The multiple-cause fallacy.
6. The overidentity of cause and effect.
7. The overriding priority fallacy.
8. The automatic solution fallacy.
9. Tautology as a cause.

It should be noted that, in logic, causes are always antecedent to the event. Something cannot have happened afterward and still be a cause. To mention this would, of course, be unnecessary if such explanations were not occasionally found. Nor does this search for antecedent events have to center on a single event. There are those who hold stoutly to the idea that the real cause of any event is the sum of *all* antecedent events and that it is wrong to pick any specific cause.[5]

The name of the game then in finding causes is to pick among the prior events and find one or several or many which seem to promise the most returns if they can be remedied, taken into account, or shunted around in the future. Let's look at the nine major fallacies within that context.

1. *The chicken-egg fallacy* is one of consciously, either in

error or for purposes of confusing the issue, declaring that cause and effect are the same thing, thus diverting attention from any constructive action for change. This is common in certain service industries and occupations. The printing industry, comprised mainly of small firms, is notable for this fallacy in its marketing and delivery methods. It begins with a sharp variation in the level of business on any particular day, and the necessity of keeping presses and workers busy during the slack times. The effect is that printing-shop owners or printing salesmen attempt to level out the volume of production by accepting orders indiscriminately, making promises they cannot possibly keep. If the printing buyer insists that he simply *must* have this "red hot" advertising brochure announcing the publication of a sensational new book for managers by Friday, urgent—he will get a promise that it will be delivered exactly then. This promise may, in fact, be totally impossible to execute since there are already eight other equally urgent orders ahead of it. Thus, the first lie is told, starting a cycle. Printing buyers with experience soon learn that printing firms are peopled by pathological liars, and so they, in turn, begin to tell whopping lies about the urgency of their own requirements. They make the date three days earlier, and insist that *this* indeed is a life-and-death priority. If, by chance, it should be completed as promised, it is left waiting for days before being picked up. The printing salesman soon realizes that his customer is a fraud and a pathological liar, so he feels no compunction about stretching the truth to any length in order to get his business. What would each state as the cause of the chaotic scheduling condition in printing sales and purchase? "The other man is a pathological liar, and therefore, I am forced to be one also."

A company's service department which provides maintenance of equipment on an "as-called" basis likewise lives in a world of promises made which will be met if convenient, and users of the service regularly lie to the department because they, in turn, have been told lies.

True understanding ensues not from information supplied by either party, but from studying the system itself, that is, identifying the kinds of promises given, and then devising order-taking and scheduling systems that will avert the necessity for lying by evening out production loads and making it possible to adhere to the schedule. The chicken-egg fallacy ordinarily entails dispersed or divided causes, camouflaged by several persons actively espousing a single cause as the truth. The pathological character of such explanations requires that some third disinterested party be involved in identifying cause and proposing corrective actions.

A variation is what logicians, always superb muddiers of the waters, call the *post hoc, ergo propter hoc* fallacy. This is the mistaken idea that if event B happened after event A, that A must have caused B. Such conclusions are the basis of superstition, such as the lady who insisted that every time she turned on her car's windshield wipers, the red lights seemed to be against her. The immediacy of an effect is often mistakenly associated casually with some coincidental and irrelevant event which occurred just prior to the event.

A few years back a family had a large collie pup who had an affinity for chewing shoes. A veterinarian advised the master of the house to cure the offending dog of the habit by striking him soundly with a newspaper the next time it occurred. Sure enough, the dog chewed up another pair of new shoes, and the master angrily looked for the dog, a rolled-up copy of the Sunday *New York Times* in hand. He came upon the dog chewing happily on a rubber bone in the laundry room. The lightning of his wrath immediately descended in the form of a resounding blow with the rolled-up newspaper. The dog never chewed a rubber bone again for the remainder of his life, being a victim of a *post hoc* fallacy.

86

While this illustration is more a product of reflex than reflective thought, it provides a good example of how the *post hoc* fallacy so easily captures us.

2. *Mixing causation and association.* This is a standard error in statistical analysis, against which every statistic book warns its readers. For example, there may be a high statistical correlation between the graduation of ministers from seminaries and the consumption of alcoholic beverages by the public. However, the causal effect may be nil, for the two phenomena are both products of a rising population and personal disposable income. Odd coincidences or meaningless relationships will always have a high statistical correlation. There seem to be three major rules which help people avert this common fallacy. Correlation alone cannot establish cause, but its absence can disestablish one. It is what logicians would call a necessary but not sufficient condition.

a. To establish cause between X and Y, there must be a *correlation*.

b. There must be a proper *temporal relationship* in their appearance; that is, cause X must have appeared sometime *before* effect Y.

c. Finally, there must be *some evidence* that connects them or provides at least presumptive proof that the relationship is more than coincidental and is causal.[6]

The behavioral scientist, having become more and more skilled as a statistician, has in recent years tended to adhere to the first two of the rules and not the third. He isolates two clusters of statistical data from his research (usually in the form of questionnaires and interviews) and finds correlations between them. For example, he finds a high correlation between loose supervision and high productivity. Because his scales are so established, this means that he must also find a high correlation between tight supervision and low productivity. Being an excellent statistician, he is satisfied by simply

87

finding such a correlation. He considers his purposes adequately completed when he produces observed associations of relationships without assigning cause and effect or other kinds of explanation to them.

Thus he can omit the second and third requirement: "I am just a pure behavioral scientist, and I don't interpret my work. I leave that to the practitioners." The fact that it might easily be misinterpreted seems only rarely to concern him. In the instance of the correlation between loose supervision and high productivity, the temporal relationship has never been clearly established. There are cases in which dictatorial managers have obtained high productivity and other cases in which they have obtained low productivity. Employees working under a restrictive supervisory style have improved after a more relaxed supervisor took over; the obverse is also true. But the temporal requirement has not been clearly established with any hard evidence. Nor has the presumptive agency between supervisory style and productivity been established, although an impression has been created by the vigor with which the causal link has been espoused. Professor Harold Levitt has suggested that the *a priori* conclusion of "power equalization" among people at work has affected the interpretation of the data.

A second kind of case is found in statistical studies of the causes of executive success. Lloyd Warner, a sociologist, has statistically studied the relationship between such factors as education and subsequent career success in business. The correlation between education and career success is high,[7] for 80 percent of the chiefs of American corporations are college graduates. A temporal relationship has also been established for, with only very few exceptions, it was always the case that they became an executive *after* they had been to college. Finally, the colleges themselves have gone to great lengths to establish the third requirement: citing such evidence as the engineering mind, the liberally trained executive, or the profes-

88

sional MBA, they have tried their utmost to establish a link.

Yet it is the third requirement that often makes absolute proof of causation impossible and places it in the area of conjecture. The Warner studies do not explain why so many noncollege men could have succeeded at the same time, nor do they cope with self-fulfilling prophecies, in which company policies, based upon earlier correlations, are written to give distinctive advantages in promotion to college graduates, thus making future correlations predictably more reliable.

Such fallacies are not confined to white-collar jobs. A large automobile company has a firm policy against promoting to the rank of foreman from the shop floor anyone who does not have at least a high school diploma. How do they know that such a level of education is necessary? Simple. They studied their present foremen and found that 80 percent of them have a high school diploma or more. What does this prove? According to their personnel man: "It proves that the odds are four to one against the nondiploma-holder's succeeding. So, why take a chance on them? They would most likely fail, so we save them that embarrassment." It may safely be predicted that, ten years from now 100 percent of their foremen will be high school graduates, thereby "proving" that only such persons are likely to be able to do the work of foremen.

An automobile dealer of my acquaintance who insists that only cigarette smokers can sell cars is the victim of such a fallacy. "How long have you known and applied this truth?" he is asked. "For twenty-five years," he replies. "And during that period, how many pipe smokers, cigar smokers, or nonsmokers have you taken on as salesmen?" "Why, none, of course. I have proof they would fail, so why bother?"

Acting on the same kind of proof, many companies hire only engineers as salesmen or college graduates as managers.

3. *Putting the effect before the cause* is a somewhat related fallacy in problem-solving. It often happens because the man

who designed the investigations and received the data back from his assistants didn't actually go out and observe what was really happening before he judged the presumptive evidence of the relationship. Take this hypothetical case:

A hospital administrator decides, for some good reason, to find out the relationship of having red-headed nurses to the body temperatures of patients in the hospital. He collects the temperature readings and, from the work assignment sheets of the chief nurse and her identification of the redheads, finds that there is a correlation between having a red-headed nurse and having a high temperature. He immediately rushes to the journals of the American Hospital Administrators with his conclusion: "Red-headed nurses cause higher temperatures."

His presumptive proof then falls into place, for he concludes that it is the exciting feminine characteristics and sparkling dynamic character of redheads (which he knows from personal experience) that causes temperatures to rise. His fallacy here is a common one in the development of presumptive proof of the causal link. *He didn't go out to the right place (where the evidence was collected) to find the presumptive proof but invented it in his office, basing it upon his own intuitions of values.* If he had gone forth in search of the presumptive proof, he would have found the following nonstatistical information:

a. The chief nurse is a grumpy old maid, now gray-haired but once a blonde, who hates redheads.

b. She always assigns redheads to the sickest patients, whose temperatures are of course the highest.

c. The correlation is a coincidence growing out of a concealed explanation not readily apparent in the numbers themselves. One might even make a case that it was the temperature which determined the chief nurse to make the assignments of the red-headed nurses rather than the other way around.

This fallacy is often perpetrated by people upon themselves.

90

The statistician merely produces the accurate numbers; the reader traps himself.

4. *The oversimplification fallacy* is that of finding a single explanation for a complex and abstract mass of information and suggesting that, if this single event occurs, then a multitude of events will follow in logical sequence and—ultimately —all is lost. Because of the nature of the management job, this search for manageable features is inescapable. If we could only find the key! This *reductive* fallacy produces several forms of error in managerial problem-solving.

a. It is often expounded by the business advocates of "free enterprise"—people who imbue the phrase with ideological significance, rather than merely defining it as a system of managing and economy. They are true believers, and clutch pamphlets from various economic education organizations, with surveys showing that schoolchildren do not believe in the profit system. They are most prone to writing letters to deans of colleges which teach economics along these lines: "I donated $100 to your Alumni Fund last year; therefore you should teach the economics of Henry George and his single-tax theory (or George Stigler, or Milton Friedman) as a means of saving the Free Enterprise System."

b. There is a confusion between the *necessary and the sufficient cause.* A company president who owned an envelope factory used to watch a single indicator to tell whether things had been going well that day: the scrap rate in the plant. "That single indicator tells me everything about how things have been going," he asserted. While the control of scrap was certainly necessary, it did not of itself make a good or bad day. However, executives often focus upon a single indicator and ride it to death. If it is bad, then a problem is automatically created. In an organization which has numerous vital signs, much as the human organism has, no single sign will give the complete cause of any condition which is unsatisfactory.

91

The sales manager who watches sales volume but neglects the costs of generating it, the ease of collecting payments after the goods are sold, and the introduction of new products into the line is a victim of a fallacy. As a result, the purposes for which the sales department was created may be only partially met. Henry Ford the elder was reported to have said, "There is no problem in this business that can't be solved by more volume." Alfred Sloan has written that it was this fixation that permitted Ford to be overtaken by General Motors, which watched consumer tastes, costs, product mix, product quality, and a host of other variables, with perhaps profitability coming closest to being their single indicator.[8]

The company that reduces the whole business to a single number will clearly find it easier to watch that number, but in the process it may have omitted handling such unintended side effects as air and water pollution or employee relations, thus finding itself in trouble. It has mistaken the necessary for the sufficient.

5. *The multiple-cause fallacy* perhaps may be considered the "staff fallacy," whereas oversimplification could be considered the "line fallacy." Despite the unfairness of such sweeping generalizations about line and staff departments, there is some evidence that staff departments such as personnel, public relations, traffic, legal, and the like have a propensity to overcomplicate the obvious. Ordinarily, such causal explanations do not state a specific number of causes, and in fact readers or listeners in staff departments wince when confronted with such statements as "there are three basic causes to this problem." Stating a single cause or a finite number of causes, such as "the ten causes of low quality" or the "seven reasons employees won't eat their lunch in the company cafeteria," is regarded as showing a *lack of sophistication.* The multiple-cause fallacy is practically epidemic in educational administration because simple, direct approaches to problems seem

revolting to the practitioners. Not only do they believe that life is vastly more complex than it seems on the surface, but also they relish the opportunity to wallow in its complexity and to make it even more so. A faculty, confronted with a simple problem such as "Shall we hand out the student awards at the banquet or the commencement convocation?" will spend days in deliberating the issue, complicating it, seeking hidden ramifications, and engaging in furious politicking and debating. Any foreman at Ford could solve it by tossing a coin. A really important problem immediately sets off a flurry of investigation of all of its ramifications, influences, relationships, factors, and sensitivities. They must think and feel about the problem on at least three levels at once: the cultural, the interpersonal, and the educational.

In management, the staff man is confronted with a natural system for complicating his thinking when he faces the complexity of the organization to which he is staff. There are product divisions, geographical divisions, and functional departments such as legal and accounting, plus a host of outside agencies to be considered.[9] Every problem, therefore, has to be considered in the light of all these interest groups, whose acceptance of a staff idea may be vital to its implementation. One staff man described the situation graphically, "It's like playing baseball on a field with eighteen bases, and you have to touch every one of them."

The necessity of such extensive minutes to get something accepted throughout the organization arises from the high costs of organization-wide error. A major error in a program affecting the entire corporation would be immensely hard to untangle. It is simpler and easier not to make it in the first place. This requires a great deal of palaver with everyone who could prevent the big error by being consulted first, all of which can easily lead to the multiple-cause fallacy and ultimate paralysis. People who have misread the real reason for

93

the complexity can make a fetish of complicating everything they touch. A staff man has been defined as someone "who sets a mole hill on his desk every morning, and spends the rest of the day making a mountain out of it." The definition illuminates the malady of multiple-causation thinking in some organizations.

6. *The overidentity fallacy* trips people who assume that there must somehow be a commonality between causes and effects which makes them somewhat similar. An example is the idea that a severe cold can be cured only by a sour-tasting medicine, whereas a minor sniffle might be fixed up with a pleasant aromatic inhaler.

Overreaction in management often grows out of this assumption. A company that was beaten out of a tremendously profitable market by a competitor as a result of a simple oversight overreacted by spending a lot of money on a beautiful research laboratory, staffed with Ph.D.s engaged in basic research, which was far too expensive for a company its size. The fallacy that big ideas must come only from big laboratories is not borne out in every case.

The oil companies have spent billions of dollars on research, but nothing comparable in import to catalytic cracking, which was invented in the 1920s, has emerged. The overreaction syndrome often arises because somebody important thinks that giant effects must always be produced by giant causes. To such a mentality, it would seem incongruous that a tick burrowing in at the wrong place can fell an ox or that a staff of forty, including engineers and nontechnical support people, could have engineered the Concorde Jet. Everyone knows that Boeing would not have laid off those thirty thousand people if it had received the contracts for the SST, so how could this be?

The fallacy of identity also catches corporations that are looking for causes of problems in one special area of the busi-

94

ness, for it traps people into assuming that production problems must have been caused in the production area, sales problems in the sales area, and so on. Because of the hardening of the categories following specialization, the sales manager is reluctant to stick his nose too far into production matters, for he will shortly be in deeper than he can handle. As a result, problems which are interdivisional or interdepartmental often simply don't get solved. The advice of the manager of department A to the manager of department B about how to solve B's problem is apt to produce little more than a sarcastic comment along these lines: "Thanks, that's just what I need—a little technical advice on how to do my job." This, of course, is a suggestion to butt out. Because this occurrence is endemic and even accepted as natural by most, the identity of problems continues to be compartmentalized.

The labor relations manager is not apt to respond favorably to suggestions from the training director that "the reason grievances are rising is because you have not trained people in the content of the labor contract." Nor are counter suggestions by the labor relations manager that "the cause of the labor problems in the plant is the sentimental, democratic management stuff being taught to the foreman by the training department" apt to produce paroxysms of enthusiasm in the training department. Thus the identity fallacy is reinforced.

7. *The overriding priority fallacy* is a frequently noted lapse is group problem-solving conferences, with the major offender being the boss. Starting with a definition of the problem and a statement of the constraints within which the solution must fit, he then becomes expansively democratic and proposes, "Now folks, let's all pitch in—I want *your* opinion." He means, of course, within the limits which he has just set upon any solutions—which is perfectly realistic if the constraints are beyond control, such as limitations of nature or customers who have resisted all appeals. They become

especially galling to the group, however, when it is known that the constraints which in effect make the problem insoluble are in reality personal idiosyncrasies of the leader.[10]

In one large midwestern firm the overriding priority that barred a solution to the problem was the condition that the firm get out of a losing line of business which the owner and founder absolutely refused to drop. The company had started in that line and had prospered in it in the past; that product had been the basis for expansion into even more profitable lines. Now that the obsolete line was a loser and a drag upon the rest of the company, the old man didn't have the slightest intention of dropping it, yet he continued to call problem-solving conferences on the subject, "How to improve the profits of the firm?"

Reports emanating from the Cabinet and National Security Council during the hottest days of the Vietnam War reveal that in several cases this overriding priority was used to avoid loss of face. In these instances, the President, the Secretary of State, and the Pentagon held the overriding priority, and any individual who proposed a full pull-out found himself clearly in a minority, working against an overriding priority reinforced by a majority of the group, supported by the top man. Such fallacious priorities comprise a limitation of the group problem-solving process.

What are the consequences of this overriding fallacy? They are not wholly bad, for the people involved are permitted to shape and control the small residue that is left to them, even after the real causes of the problem have been debarred. The converse, though, is also true. If they have been forced to accept as the true cause something which is irrelevant or tangential to the problem, then acceptance of a wrong solution is probably likelier than it might have been, and wrong choices will be efficiently executed.

A product of living with the overriding fallacy on a chronic basis is that a special maneuver of the activity trap called *fighting the problem* emerges. Rather than pitching in and working at solutions, the group may suggest that the problem is not really a problem but a figment of somebody's imagination, or else they may ask for what the lawyers call a change of venue, which means moving the problem to some other jurisdiction. "Let's send it over to the accounting department and see what they can do with it" or "Those personnel people are always making big pronouncements about their knowledge of human relations—let's dump this one in their lap." Another way of fighting the problem is to presume that conditions which can never exist will shortly come into being: "When they pass the new tax bill (or when the tax rebate comes through or when the Fed eases up on the money crunch), then *that* will solve the problem and we won't have to waste our time and energy solving it."

Fighting problems is such a natural defense against the painful decisions in solving problems that it is not surprising it is so common. Even the best get caught at it.

Arthur D. Little, one of the leading companies in research and consulting, had a rough year in 1971, as did many in that industry. Earnings and volume were down sharply from the year before. In explaining the problem, chairman James H. Gavin confessed to a moderate amount of problem-fighting. "We carried some people who had nothing much to do for about a year waiting for that turnaround the Nixon people kept talking about, but we couldn't wait forever," he was reported to have said in *Business Week* in November. While the company paid 100 people for not working, management apparently fought the problem. It was not the company, its sales force, or management who would solve the problem, but Nixon. The most redeeming feature of this example is that management recognized what they were doing and halted it before heavier losses occurred.[11]

A further ill effect of habitual use of the overriding priority fallacy is that it develops cynicism about use of the group

97

problem-solving process itself and results in the feeling or realization that one is being manipulated. That is, the individual is being given verbal assurances that his participation in problem-solving is desired, while in fact he is receiving palliatives, the real core of the decision-making being retained by the boss.

8. *The automatic solution fallacy* has grown rapidly in the age of the computer. This marvelous instrument has indeed permitted the solution by mechanical and automated methods of many problems which previously required independent human judgments. The possibilities for removing many areas of problem-solving and decision-making from human judgment are appealing. The computer can collect, classify, sort data, compare with predetermined standards, and announce differences.[12] These functions are what much of human involvement in problem-solving and decision-making has consisted of in the past and are probably what Simon Ramo had in mind in the fifties when he accurately predicted that some day management decisions would be automated.[13] Yet, as a blanket assumption, this reliance upon automatic decision-making has several fallacies to be avoided.

a. The computer cannot define its own standards, for this is a function of those who define objectives of the organization. Such objectives may include such nonroutine goals as providing a job for the owner's son even though he doesn't contribute very much, avenging a dirty deal pulled by the fellow down the street, and impressing your brother-in-law that you are more prosperous than you really are.

b. The computer (or the operations research program) is far better at treating the various components of a system as though they were detachable and independently operative than at treating them all at once in unique combinations. The computer, in other words, is not as good at compromising and finding middle-ground solutions as people are.

98

Take the case of Mr. Smith, the men's haberdasher who joined a trade association and placed data covering all of his important accounting and business variables into a computer operated by it. He sent over a night wire the weekly results of his store. The computer would then automatically add and subtract these figures and produce a new position statement which came back by return mail on Monday morning. The owner would then know exactly where he stood with respect to cash position, inventory volumes by categories, markup gains, receivables, reorder signals, and a host of other decisions which ordinarily occupy most of the time of the small merchant. One Monday the computer informed Mr. Smith that his inventory build-up in certain items was rising too fast and that he should stop reordering those items and immediately cut prices by 20 percent and run a big clearing-out sale to convert his surplus inventory into cash. It even suggested that he refer to his master file and pull out the details of conducting such a campaign, including sample advertising copy, signs to be painted for the windows, and several other merchandising ideas he could follow. Mr. Smith, however, knew that he was not going to comply, for his store was located near a college and it would be opening in two weeks. He wanted those inventory items for that opening, besides which he had plenty of cash from a slight "killing" he had made on a real estate deal. By ignoring the instructions, he made more money than if he had slavishly followed them. Did it mean the computer was wrong? Not at all. It had given him valid information, based upon the data available to it, which Mr. Smith's common sense told him he had better ignore. He remembered the extra cash and set it aside for use in averting the potential problem the computer had warned him about. He also used his own memory rather than the computer's to test whether or not he should unload inventory at lower prices, and decided against it.

The computer can be a teaching machine for managers if they will learn from it. For example, if there are nine elements in a decision which needs to be made to solve a problem, it does not mean that only one of the nine contains the major cause. Perhaps combinations of four or five, or all nine, can be creatively synthesized. While it is theoretically possible for computers to program any number of combinations, in practice these programs are simplified to save expensive computer time. There still remains much room for imaginative human action.

9. A final reason problems don't get solved is that sometimes people treat *the fact as a cause of itself*. As explained in Chapter 3, it is tautological to say that something equals itself. While it is impossible to dispute the accuracy of such a statement, it is unlikely to be useful in finding solutions. President Calvin Coolidge once explained unemployment in a true but meaningless form: "When large numbers of people cannot find work, the result is unemployment." Unemployment and people not being able to find work have an identity that bars their being considered in a cause-and-effect relationship.

A closely related variation of this fallacy occurs when two related events in time are tied together as cause and effect. "Joe died because he was hit by a truck." Indisputably, as his grieving heirs can testify, Joe has gone to his reward, but it would be perfectly accurate to state that "Joe was hit by a truck and died of his injuries." To be hit by a truck is not in every case a cause of death. Nobody disputes that getting hit by trucks is generally not a salubrious pastime, but in some cases the victim gets up and castigates the driver or he is injured but recovers or he simply lies there and calls for a lawyer. Nonetheless, the logical lapse is a common one, even more so in complex problems.

It is equally diverting and damaging to the problem-solving process to confuse the source of the facts in the problem with

100

the empirical and reliable data itself. Take the case of a large airliner that is flying at 35,000 feet and suddenly hits some clear air turbulence (CAT). It throws the plane about; the passengers are tossed around with food and drink and articles of hand luggage; and there are some minor injuries. An investigation reveals the following data:

Source	Explanatory Statements
Pilot	"We operate at levels where CAT can occur without warning, which is why we suggest that passengers keep their seat belts fastened at all times."
Stewardess	"Every time I start to serve drinks, it gets choppy."
Passenger	"Gee, I just pushed the stewardess-call button, and bang, the whole plane leaped. I guess I hit the emergency brakes."

None of the statements is false, but they originate from persons of differing viewpoints and perceptions. Stories of battles vary greatly—apparently nobody, not even the generals who presumably are in command, really can tell what is going on. The same phenomena occur in business. The Bell System is reported to have 985,000 employees in cities, villages, and towns across the nation, and as such it is highly unlikely that the entire truth about the telephone company can emerge in a single piece. For the individual subscriber, the telephone company is picking up the instrument on his desk and dialing Mother—and reaching her or getting some disturbance. A thousand others have a thousand other facts.

The complexity of the environment is the best argument for getting the problem-solving process down to the lowest possible level, where the person who sees a problem is authorized to act toward its solution.

101

Chapter 6

When the Facts Go
Into Hiding

*In activity-centered organizations, facts
often go into hiding.*

ONCE I HAD TO INTRODUCE A CORPORATION PRESIDENT as the speaker at a large conference. Eager to do a good job, I called his office and asked his secretary for some biographical information. She referred the request to an assistant, who in turn called the public relations department. There it was referred to the speaker's bureau. The information was relayed back along the line, and I obtained it over the telephone. In order that it be accurate, I asked my secretary to take notes from the description given by the speaker's secretary. I introduced the estimable gentleman, and he acknowledged my introduction about as follows:

"I am flattered by this kind introduction. There are a few modifications in fact, however. I didn't go to Indiana. I went to Illinois. I didn't serve in the army, but in the navy. I am not chairman, but president and chief executive officer of my company. I didn't start in sales, but in manufacturing. However, I am flattered to be invited."

102

All of which spoke well of his good nature and kindly disposition, and of the difficulty in obtaining accurate facts when they are passed from one person to another.

The Elusive Nature of Fact

If ten witnesses, all with unobstructed views, see the same event, they can be depended upon to report at least three—and perhaps even ten—versions of the event. It gets more difficult to ascertain facts as they increase in complexity. Deriving facts from what remains of the event, we try to reconstruct it from other direct evidence (observations of witnesses) and from circumstantial evidence (related facts that indicate what happened). The further we get from the event itself, the greater the probability of losing the truth.

The boss may easily be excused for not seeing everything that goes on if he has 50,000 employees spread all over the map making a thousand products for millions of customers. Since he cannot be expected to know everything at first hand, he nearly always has to rely on what somebody, designated to get the facts, tells him. And that informant, in turn, usually must rely to a considerable extent on what others tell him.

Of course, when people tell things, they don't always tell the truth, the whole truth, and so forth. Very often it is to somebody's advantage not to tell all. Not every boss takes kindly to bad news, and it's not always smart to play true confessions about your own shortcomings. The Turkish proverb, "The messenger bringing bad news should keep one foot in the stirrup" is still heard.

An old fable tells of a mouse that constantly tried to impress an elephant, but to no avail. One day, however, he got through to him.

"Look, Mr. Elephant, see how the clouds float across the sky, thereby causing the wind to blow." The elephant opened one eye.

103

"See, also, this little bamboo shoot. Someday it will grow up to become a mighty mahogany tree." The other eye opened.

The elephant was apparently impressed with this wisdom. "Where do you get your facts?" he asked.

"I make them up!" said the mouse.

Many a mouse in this world has made up facts to impress some elephant of his fancy. Young men embellish their adventures to impress ladies of their choice. People seeking power or money or love or merely a slight advantage find that facts are malleable. We bend them to give ourselves an advantage, to prevent pain or inconvenience, or to avoid hurting another whose opinion is important. We shape them to avoid arousing wrath in those whose ill will we fear. The credibility of witnesses can be a function of their interests as well as their morals.

But there is often a more fundamental reason why subordinates don't level with the boss: they themselves simply don't know. The truth often eludes people even when the evidence is before their eyes because they don't understand what comprises evidence or are not able correctly to assess its significance. A man is sent out to find the facts, and he goes right to the spot where causes, consequences, and witnesses of the event are evident in liberal quantities; yet he comes back and reports something that is largely unfactual!

Nevertheless, the truth occasionally does emerge—mainly because it's *there* at each level of perception, and careful investigation and logical use of evidence may help bring it forth. If we recognize the brambles where facts can hide, we may be able to flush them out.

It is possible to identify at least six ways (there are countless variations) in which facts can be hidden in an organization:

1. The Chicken Little Fallacy (The Missing Connection).
2. Reversible Evidence (The Rear-View Fact).

104

3. Irrelevant Evidence ("Here's the Answer, What's the Question?")
4. Ghost Proof (Negative Proof of Affirmative Facts).
5. The Hot Potato Proof (Buck Passing).
6. The Figure-Eight Indictment.

1. *The Chicken Little Fallacy* (*The Missing Connection*). Sometimes people dash breathlessly into the boss's office to announce a *fact*. What they have is a piece of evidence, quite verifiable. From this, they jump to a conclusion (often plausible, perhaps even defensible, but not *proved*) which they treat as a hard fact.

When Chicken Little was struck on the head by a small falling object, she dashed forth to announce that "the sky is falling," and as a by-product lent her name to this trap. The evidence was factual, but her conclusion was specious. It has been said of her that "she announced her findings before her research was complete." Not an uncommon event.

Take the case of the editor of a liberal newspaper who was conducting a running verbal battle with a leading industrialist. The tycoon was known to be strongly opposed to liberal causes. When a new housing development for low-income families was proposed, the editor determined to throw the full resources of his paper behind the new program. He assigned his star reporter to cover it. After a couple of days of digging in, the reporter came up with a nugget of fact: the industrialist, only two weeks before, had signed a petition opposing a piece of legislation favoring labor union organizations. The paper, the next day, published this as evidence that he was a leader in opposition to low-income housing. Immediately, the tycoon denied the charge and demanded an apology. He was, he declared, strongly in favor of low-income housing. "But he can't be!" complained the reporter. "A man who is opposed to labor legislation must be opposed to housing for the poor

105

as well!" Nonetheless, the paper published a retraction under threat of a libel suit. The editor and his reporter were victims of faulty logic.

The old saying "Where there's smoke, there's fire" doesn't mean that every whiff proves a new Chicago fire. Yet many a witness has dashed upstairs to report such a conflagration as a fact! A boss having to rely on someone could be misled.

There is always the possibility that people will fly in the face of their own past practices. The Conservative Party candidate for the Presidency of the United States was reported to have been on the conservative side in his congressional voting record on 96 percent, not 100 percent, of the issues;[1] this meant that even this paragon deviated 4 percent of the time.

In a large eastern factory the union was quite disturbed because a new young supervisor made a practice of jumping in and doing manual work. The labor contract explicitly forbade the practice, and union leaders complained bitterly to higher management. The brass agreed that the man was wrong and admonished him against any repetition. All was well for some time; then one day the shop chairman walked into the big boss's office. "I've got a beef about a foreman doing union work," he stated. Immediately the boss flew into a rage and, rushing out of the office, he collared the past offender and dressed him down in front of a number of people, then fumed his way back into his office. There he found the union officer, who informed him coolly: "Wrong man. It was one of your old-timers on another floor."

Even respectable scientists can slip into similar fallacies when they write about management research. In an otherwise superior book, *Research Among Animals*, Dr. Harry Levinson of the Menninger Clinic shows that, when individual males of the same species fight with each other, there is a high death rate among losers, even where the injuries are not the

106

cause of death. From this he concludes that direct competition between individuals "where one is clearly the victor and the other is a loser, is literally destructive of life."[2] This excellent, scholarly book is marred by an isolated example of the fallacy of overgeneralization from sparse evidence. An investigation of Dr. Levinson's source shows it to be a study by L. S. Ewing, "Fighting and Death from Stress in a Cockroach," *Science*, February 1967. Is one study of cockroaches sufficient evidence for asserting that competition *between executives* in which there are winners and losers is destructive of life?

A comparable leap in logic is demonstrated in an article by Fred Fiedler, "The Effect of Intergroup Competition on Group Member Adjustment."[3] Here, a study of consistently losing athletic teams becomes the basis for a generalization that can be taught to nascent businessmen as a guide to their behavior. Unfortunately, far too much behavioral research on business management is characterized by such fallacies. In part this happens because behavioral scientists are far less careful in checking the design of experiments and the interpretation of data by their peers than are the "hard" scientists.

When *indications* are treated as *proof*, some humility in generalization is called for.

Many behavioral science studies move too readily from bit to grand theory, leading one to suspect that the fact to be proved may have been in hand and that the research was designed to provide hard indicators of its veracity.[4] Studies consisting of interviews with 238 engineers are the basis for a series of hard prescriptions about how *all* people want to be treated. Telephone calls to two thousand homes are the source for assumptions (treated partially as facts) as to how seventy million viewers like a television show. Even conceding power to scientific statistical analysis, there is much to be concerned about in the generalizations that affect us.

2. *Reversible Evidence (The Rear-View Fact)*, too, can

help people hide the facts from everyone, including themselves. This fallacy involves citing an event *after* the supposed fact to prove the existence of the fact. This "proof" is often taken as attaching guilt to some person, such as a responsible staff member or a careless bungler, or even as explaining old mysteries in terms of contemporary evidence.

The fact that man has a vermiform appendix is proof that he once had a tail, that is, another vestigial appendage.

The fact that a company suffered a serious business reverse in 1972 proves that its officers "probably had faked the true situation in the year 1971 figures," thus making their incompetence in that earlier year a matter of fact, even if it was invisible and nonexistent in 1971.

The fact that tonight your son, John, came home with the smell of beer on his breath is proof that he has been carousing with those gangs in the beer-busts which the police have been trying to break up for the past month.

The fact that in 1970 the president of a large and troubled automobile company was fired for conflict of interests proves that the operations of the company had been corrupt all the way back to 1964, when its profits started to decline.

However plausible the idea or tempting the gossip, it was not a hard fact.

3. *Irrelevant Evidence* (*"Here's the Answer, What's the Question?"*) is another way people use rationality to miss actuality and consists of taking a set of facts as evidence in a matter to which they are not relevant.

Shortly after a new owner took over a New Jersey factory he was obliged to fire four employees hired prior to his regime who were falsifying their time cards. A couple of weeks later his Washington sales office reported that a discrepancy in billing had appeared in a customer's account.

"Do you have any salesmen left from the old work force?" the president snapped. Informed that there was one such

108

person, the president ordered him fired. The reason? (The boss already had an answer for questions not yet asked.) "He's one of those old-timers, and I've found them to be untrustworthy!"

Thus the factual evidence of wrongdoing by the old-timers in the factory in New Jersey became "proof" of the dishonesty of the salesman in Washington.

4. *Ghost Proof (Negative Proof of Affirmative Facts)* is an attempt to sustain an affirmative fact by means of negative evidence.

Take the case of the consultant who was hired to assess the quality of performance of a large group of managers and professionals. The consultant reported: "We have studied the records of the past several years of the plant and have found not a single shred of evidence that Mr. Hamilton and his crew have made any affirmative contributions, and thus we recommend that he and his group be released for not having contributed anything."

In still another instance, a school board was requested to discharge a librarian because "there is no evidence that she showed a favorable attitude toward helping students in their research, and her job demands such an attitude. Thus, we conclude that her attitude is deficient, and she should be released." Of course, what was missing here was any positive evidence of a bad attitude, and so the ousting group used negative evidence. Perhaps, you may say, the librarian really did have a bad attitude. Perhaps. But no evidence was produced and apparently none was found.

Some further examples would include these statements:

"We receive no complaints from employees, so we know they are satisfied with their jobs." (Perhaps they are too frightened or miserable to complain.)

"In twenty years no author has ever protested that we have reviewed his work unfairly, thus demonstrating our meticulous

109

scholarship and impartiality." (Perhaps they have been unduly flattering or overly generous—they may even have let the authors write their own reviews.)

5. *The Hot Potato Proof (Buck Passing)*. This fallacy rests on *presumptive* proof, while trying to place on others the burden of disproving something, usually a charge of misfeasance or nonfeasance.

"The dissident stockholders call upon the management to prove the accuracy of their accounting and financial statements over the past five years."

"I think you are guilty of some kind of hank-panky and if you can't prove otherwise, then it must be presumed to be a fact."

Marshall McLuhan, the master of the put-on in the age of electronics, has constructed an entire system of nonproof built on aphorisms, quips, and outrageous assertions. Asked what evidence he relies on for his firmly stated conclusions, he replied, "I let the listener try to make his own sense of what I say."[5]

For years business and financial writers have soberly represented similar kinds of arrant nonsense as fact. With regard to prices on the New York Stock Exchange on the Wednesday before Thanksgiving 1971, the *New York Times* declared that "the market benefited from some short coverings by traders planning a long weekend."[6] So, if you wanted to know why Bausch and Lomb moved up 2⅝ to 137⅜ or IBM added 1¼ to 291¾, you were told it was because the dealers in these stocks were covering short to protect themselves while they were driving north to close the summer place. If you don't believe it, ask them. The onus lies on you.

The proposition that the reporter, V. G. Vartan, actually checked the holiday weekend plans of the traders to prove his assertion is, of course, absurd. It is a convention of financial reporting to give some reason—any reason—why the market did what it did. Any concurrent event will do to explain any

110

change in any direction. The burden of proof lies with the reader, even if he suspects that it's pure puffery. "If you think that's not the reason, prove that it *isn't* the reason!" would be a sensible retort, and you are left holding the bag. Since practically nobody really believes such causal statements about stock market fluctuation reports anyhow, little if any harm is done.

6. *The Figure-Eight Indictment* is a fallacy in which the facts run in circles.

"The most effective organizations are those where the boss is permissive. This management style, being the most productive, permits more freedom to subordinates to apply their talents." Thus goes the conclusion of a behavioral scientist on the question of what style of supervision produces the highest employee productivity.

What's wrong with his conclusion? For one thing, the question of fact is begged and the assumption turned into a conclusion. Was it the high productivity which led the boss to loosen his management controls, or was it the loose controls which induced the high productivity? The statement and the accompanying explanation give no hint. The two are clearly associated in the evidence. That A causes B or that B causes A cannot be accepted on the strength of mere assumption and assertion; what is required is more explanatory evidence of the relationship.

"High profits and a strong research and development department accompany one another. This contribution of research to stockholder benefits is thus a reliable fact of modern corporate life." Did the high profits produce a strong research department, or did the strong research department produce the high profits? Or were both the product of some concealed fact not mentioned? One cannot tell from the statement. Perhaps both grew out of a lucky accident or a strong marketing program.

A variant of the figure-eight proof is that of begging the

111

question. The question is posed, then assumed to be true, or perhaps is "proved" to be true on the basis of an unproven assumption.

A recent book by Robert Heller, *The Great Executive Dream*, is laden with witty and skeptical judgments, which incidentally provide numerous examples of question-begging. For example, he suggests that greed is the greatest motivator in all its forms.

The question: Are executives motivated by greed?

Research: Executives always seem to be seeking money, bonuses, or nonfinancial benefits which can't be disentangled from money.

Tacit assumption: Greed consists of wanting something, either financial or nonfinancial, very badly.

Conclusion: Businessmen are greedy.

If you accept the tacit assumption, so are concert pianists, ministers of state, and the majority of saints.

The book is written in journalistic style and seems intended more for provocation than presentation of facts. And it will certainly jar the executive reader, partly because of the half-truths it contains and even more because of its frequent resort to circular proof. Some typical quotes:

"In management, wonders nearly always cease!"

"The average performance of big companies is just that, average."

"There are no theories of growth . . . there are only actions, intelligent, not so bright, and stupid."[7]

The assertive writing and epigrammatic language make it attractive both to business and executive readers as well as the general public. In the first two of the three quotations, the circularity is in the form of tautology. The third is question-begging.

COMMENTS ON FACT-GATHERERS

1. The manager who sends people on a fact-gathering expedition would be well-advised to expect the safari to return with more than facts, something other than facts, as well as some hard factual information. People return with such a mixed bag because their interests lie in finding what they did find rather than the facts they did not find.

2. Regarding readiness to find or accept facts that point to the necessity for change and innovation, people can be distributed along a curve with three populations on it: (a) At the bottom, a small group of those who will violently resist any change, however slight, and will continue to resist indefinitely, perhaps pathologically, at an ascending rate of resistance. (b) At the top, a small group of temperamental, chronic rebels who not only want to change everything but, as soon as their new proposal is adopted, will want to change that as well. (c) In the middle, the great majority, who will change when they can see quite clearly that there are advantages for them in the changes and disadvantages for them in things remaining as they are.

3. It is not to be expected that technical information will change the attitudes of people where such attitudes have deep cultural and social roots. Facts are often merely the bricks by which one builds proofs of one's cultural biases.[8]

113

Chapter 7

<hr>

The Information Overload

<hr>

In activity-centered organizations the provision of data is inversely related to comprehension of reality.

MANAGERIAL DECISION-MAKING IS A SELECTION PROCESS. Given facts, opportunities, threats, problems, risks, strengths, and weaknesses of relative positions, the executive makes his decisions. In the modern corporation and government agency, it is increasingly likely that this decision-making will be by some kind of consensus. General Motors has for decades operated through its key policy and administration committees.[1] The executive seems to be moving more in the direction of becoming the operator of decision-making machines rather than making personal decisions. The National Security Council and the Joint Chiefs of Staff in the military sift data and opinions to produce decisions, or, to be more precise, alternatives from among which the Chief Executive may choose.

In earlier chapters we saw how difficult it can be to find facts in view of all the possible pitfalls. Even where the boss selectively sends others out to gather facts, he should be skeptical. What he receives from them may or may not depict the actual situation accurately and comprehensively. Information, yes—probably masses of it. A simple, clear-cut, sufficiently complete representation of reality? Almost never. Confronted with data from which it is difficult to extract significance, management has a natural tendency to move slowly, maintain the status quo, or perhaps retreat to a previously prepared position. Thus the activity trap tightens its grip on the higher councils of the organization.

From the outside, information flows in from such sources as customers, consultants, market research, and government agencies. Within the organization, information moves upward from lower levels. The inside process isn't a simple one, although it has been simply described by Kenneth Boulding: "The reports flow up and the vetoes flow down."

One of the newest attempts at coping with the problem is called the *Management Information System* (MIS). This is the province of experts in computers, data-processing systems, and the most up-to-date information-transmission equipment. The costs of information are becoming astronomical; to install MIS costs millions. For example, Ford Motor Company is reported to be spending hundreds of thousands of dollars each day for leased telephone lines through which its many computers talk to one another. An essential feature of the MIS system is a *data bank*, in which facts are stored for ready access by the individual decision-maker or the decision-making team.

Why Data Banks Are a Boondoggle

The data bank has great potential value, but in actual practice, overall, it has some unfortunate effects. The enormous mass of information is assembled for reluctant executives by suspicious and hostile subordinates. In the process, the forces favoring retention of present systems are strengthened, while those fostering innovation are weakened. MIS, in effect, becomes part of the activity trap.

115

The sources of most data are the lower levels in the organization, and these sources are almost invariably firmly committed to present procedures. It is hardly surprising, then, that *most data is intended for control and maintenance of the existing system.* Innovation never comes through cost accounting, quality control, or other maintenance procedures. These useful, necessary systems merely maintain the status quo. Innovation comes through new ideas, a commodity which as yet no control procedure, data bank, or Management Information System has been able to produce.

The strength and continuity of the activity trap is powerfully fostered by the numerous pitfalls that lie before an individual or committee attempting to extract significance from data. Five major sources of bloopers by management in interpreting data, in addition to flaws in the data itself, can be listed:

1. Bosses are inundated with more information than they could possibly use.

2. High-level management tends to see only the total picture—to see things wholly and globally.

3. They mistake the essence of the issue.

4. They worship measurement.

5. They hate measurement and adore the vague.

This array of difficulties, coupled with the dubious quality of much of the data and the need for consensus among group decision team members, constitutes a sizable obstacle to change. How do these logical improprieties occur in practice? Let's look at each in some detail.

1. *Too much information.* Professor Russell Ackoff[2] has pointed out that it is a popular myth that managers, by getting more information than they now receive, will thereby make better decisions. Rather, they would be burdened with the necessity of discarding quantities of nonessential material. Perfunctory screening, understandable in view of the manager's

desire to save time, may permit valuable nuggets of information to wind up in the slag heap. A further disadvantage is that, after screening, the data must be rearranged in the order of importance. (Ackoff proposes that a *model* of the firm is required to achieve sound information management.)

Two classes of management information can be identified. *Control* information, having to do with deviations from standards, is, as consultant Joseph Juran has pointed out, mainly designed to maintain the status quo. The other type is information that can be used creatively.

Control entails comparison with some standard. The actual results are compared with the standards and the differences highlighted. These differences come to the attention of the higher-level manager, who presumably then may issue orders remedying the variation, thereby returning the process to control.[3] Such feedback systems, which are the basis of quality control, production control, and almost all accounting systems, do nothing to change the character of things but, in fact, are highly sophisticated instruments to enforce the activity trap. They correct deviation and restore normality; they focus attention on control rather than innovation, and make no provision for the expenditure of time or energy for exploitation of new opportunities or introduction of change. Yet control information is necessary, of course. Innovative programs without controls create dangerous instability.

How much and what kind of control information should be filtered upward? The exception principle provides an answer.[4] Not all information about departures from accepted standards need be reported to the manager. One corrective to mindless heaping up of nonessential information on the manager's desk is to have some subordinate exercise a measure of self-control. At the beginning of each operating period, he and his boss could agree upon objectives, including the levels of excellence and of unsatisfactory output. When exceptions occur, he

117

would be authorized to take action and, where necessary, to consult with his superior. Such a self-control system gives the subordinate considerable freedom without leaving him adrift, and at the same time frees the top people for more innovative, creative, and developmental work.[5]

Ironically, even when freed for creative thinking and strategic planning, top people often fail to field imaginative ideas properly because they overlook the innovative potentials in the received information. They persist in obtaining *operational* information in far more detail than is needed. The end result is that operating-results information crowds out the information needed for growth, change, and improvement. Because the raw material of new ideas looks quite ordinary, its significance may not be grasped.

2. *Trying to see the whole thing.* For decades, the four-week management courses of the American Management Association have been well attended. One of the more popular segments in the final week has been the session on "see it big—keep it simple" (leading, in the spirit of the thing, to the acronym SIBKIS). The principle is that the top man must see the organization or company as an entity rather than as specific parts. It is plausible enough that the top man must be able to generalize across all units, but SIBKIS in its detailed workings must be recognized as absurd. How can one see everything without seeing anything? Calls for extreme generalization espouse ignorance. Sadly, those who have tried to apply it report, as did the man in the television commercial, "I can't believe I ate the whole thing!"

It is quite proper to suggest that strategy must start at the top. But strategic planning involves intensive scrutiny of the organization in numerous particulars—where it is trending, what its opportunities, strengths, weaknesses, problems, threats, risks, and objectives might be. Without such specifics, it would be impossible to judge such matters as organization values.[6] Of

118

course it is wrong for top management to be overly attentive to day-by-day operational events, especially if such details can be delegated by following the exception principle. But it is not wrong—indeed it is essential—for top management to be aware of major facts with a bearing upon strategic opportunities for change and improvement.

Jan Christiaan Smuts originated the term *holism*, which has been widely adopted to describe this emphasis on grasping a thing in its entirety.[7] In economics, in history, and in management, such a concept serves mainly to confuse. As applied to management information systems, it means that the top people select their facts as determined by "the sense of the whole" rather than by some other criteria for what is significant.

Holistic thinking occurs frequently in the management of high talent manpower. The liberal arts graduate is inculcated with the notion that his broad education qualifies him to oversee narrow specialists.[8] Graduates of top business colleges are often persuaded that they have sufficient knowledge about business in general to manage an entire company, even though they couldn't manage any single segment of it. An MBA degree from certain prestigious schools virtually guarantees a man that he may never have to work at an unrewarding level if he is lucky enough to land in the management training program of one of the larger corporations. His salary progress will be faster than that of the man without such a degree, his appraisals better, his promotions more rapid—in many instances, without having his *performance* tested. This is not to suggest that MBA's are unqualified for employment or that it is a mistake to hire them. On the contrary, they really do have, in my experience, the best education for business and managerial careers. Occasionally, they have even learned decision-making and problem-solving skills superior to those of the present generation of managers. But their generalist skills should not be regarded as permitting them to do *nothing*. The best generalist is not the one who generalizes on the basis of ignorance of everything.

Generalizing is best done by the person who knows everything about everything, not the person who knows nothing about everything.

3. *The search for essence.* Inseparably linked with the attempt to generalize is a search for the essence of things, the heart of the issue. It is a compliment to say of an executive, "he has a true capacity to get to the heart of the issue" in his discussions with subordinates. The idea here is that amidst the confusing welter of opinions and data there is a centrum of real meaning—the profound, all-explaining core of the whole mishmash.

Such an approach is the basis of much analytical work. The application of such guides as Pareto's law, a widely employed analytical tool, is in effect a search for the vital few among the trivial many. Pareto was an economist who found that there was a normal, natural maldistribution between causes and effects that could be described statistically. Ordinarily, he noted, things distribute themselves in a 20 to 80 ratio—that is, 80 percent of the effects can be attributed to 20 percent of the possible causes. According to his law, for example, about 20 percent of the employees will account for about 80 percent of the absenteeism. Knowing the validity of this principle, a manager can use it as a tool for plunging through masses of data to essences. Rather than frittering away his time on that part of the data which could have no payback in increased output, he identifies and concentrates on the vital 20 percent.[9]

Charles Kepner and Benjamin Tregoe have developed a most useful exercise, designed to teach managers how to make decisions and solve problems. While the model for this exercise is too complex to state in a few words, it, too, represents a method for helping managers find essences. One feature of the course is the use of the question "Is—is not?" when confronted by complex and often self-contradictory information. By analyzing the problem into polar opposites, the essence can be quickly reached. Once the first round of questioning is done, the whole mass of possibilities has been reduced by 50 percent. After the second round, the data residue becomes 25 percent of the original.[10] (This device is somewhat akin to "twenty questions," a game played on panel shows on television during the 1950s.)

The catch with such devices is that they may prove to be mirrors into which the manager is staring with great satisfaction rather than—as he supposes—windows into the inner workings of the firm and its problems. Having chosen an analytical tool which seems to promise ultimate explanations of everything, the management analyst uses it and comes up with an opinion that seems miraculously to express the essence. The acceptance is high for the conclusion, and the energy of the organization in implementing such decisions is encouragingly high. The search for essences is an important part of the mystique of Operations Research, which reduces the entire organization to a mathematical model—the purest of essences according to its advocates.[11]

The Academy of Management, an organization of management professors, is deeply immersed in seeking a fundamental or general theory of management.[12] In their talent hunt for a Keynes in the management field, they have filled their journal with papers stressing new approaches to general management theory. Likewise, the behavioral scientists, through questionnaires and interviews, have sought an essential theory of employee motivation. Likert suggests that it should be based on management styles, with participative and supportive management being the essence. Maslow asserts that self-actualization provides the highest levels of motivation. In a more recent book, Harry Levinson suggests that Maslow is wrong and that the essence is realization of "ego ideal."[13]

The search for such an essence has almost irresistible appeal

121

to the manager. Isolated in many cases from the raw data of the organization, he is flooded with information every time he tries to find reality. Small wonder that he looks for simplifying assumptions.

The search for essences will fail without wide knowledge of the entire organization. Essence cannot be discovered or recognized by the person who knows little or nothing about everything.

4. *The worship of measurable facts.* For many managers at the top, the only viable way of coping with the information overload is to reduce all information to numbers. For the number-worshiper, if a thing can't be reduced to numbers, it doesn't exist; and, of course, if it doesn't exist, then there is no point in wasting anybody's valuable time in discussing it. The fallacy lies in going to such extremes. Every rational person quantitates where possible and useful. To count one's children when heading home from a picnic is an act of love, not a depersonalization. In managing information, an indispensable way to achieve understanding is to sort new data into classes, then to array these in scales, and finally to define mathematical relationships between the classes and clusters.[14]

This procedure is somewhat different from that of the figure-worshiper who takes over much managerial decision-making at the top. He is a deluded victim of the *quantitative fallacy*, according to which the *significance of data is in proportion to its quantitation.* For him, what cannot be quantified is irrelevant—the relevance of data is determined to the degree to which it can be quantified.

The rising importance of accounting as a decision-making tool can, in part, be explained by the trend to measurability as the sole criterion of significance of data. More and more accountants have moved into top management positions, at least partly because of the belief that people who can cope with quantitation must be able to see significance in the masses of information produced in a modern corporation. When the president of a major corporation was asked what his objectives were, he replied, "To make the numbers." Although the sample is small, my own survey of what presidents see as true corporate objectives shows that most do see the numbers as the only significant goal. After the numbers come other values, such as social responsibility.

The growth of operations research has been an incidental but important beneficiary of this fallacious overreliance on measurement. While the operations researcher emphasizes that his contributions lies not just in data collection but even more in model-making and analytical methods, his acceptance by management has been quick chiefly because he is seen as a staff person who can provide quantitative proof ("hard data") when the company is faced with tough management problems, such as plant location or product mix.

Of course, the antimeasurement clique who would dismiss all quantitation as being contrary to the human spirit goes too far. What the author advocates is not to avoid numbers but to avoid attaching undue weight to a fact merely because it is *expressed* in numerical form. The criteria by which executives must screen facts as to significance are substantive in nature, not numerical.

Take the case of the firm that made a managerial decision to initiate a Management by Objectives (MBO) Program. The managers and staff participated enthusiastically. In addition to stating a goodly number of objectives for the control of financial, sales, and manufacturing figures, they also added a number of highly innovative and invaluable programs dealing with improved public relations, employee relations, and product and customer service. At the end of the year, the results were reviewed by the top management officials. When the rewards and citations for achievement were issued, it became very clear that only those goals which had measurable outcomes were being recognized. Among those which had been left unrecognized was a complete turnaround of the community's attitude from hostile to friendly and supportive. A general decline in employee hostility was another salutary but unrecognized outcome.

Furthermore, everyone knew that the manager who had come off best in the MBO results sweepstakes had actually done the company considerable damage by the way in which he had obtained the splendid numerical results in his plant. For one thing, he had badly injured labor relations by breaking faith with union officers during the year. Each of these labor leaders made known his intent to "get even" with the company for betrayals at the hands of this manager. A second negative accomplishment which did not appear on the numerical results table worshiped so ardently by top management was the destruction of the careers of two promising young men who had been in his baleful area of influence. Both had been forced from the company for no other offense than that they were sufficiently competent to threaten the manager's own progress. Still another devastating result which did not appear on any account book was his practice with regard to maintenance of the equipment under his control. By cutting necessary repairs during the year, he had shown impressive "savings." Needless to say, the costs in downtime and poor quality in following years exceeded by far what he had "saved."

High-level management often assumes erroneously that the full effect of measurable efforts will be visible during the year in which the effort was expended, but many highly important results are gradual. The expenditures for a Veterans' Administration hospital may not have an immediate one-year payback, but over five years may more than return to the government its first-year expenditures, in tax income from rehabilitated veterans.

124

In their decision-making processes, the manager and the management committee are sometimes too concise. They receive information in numerical form, and publish their decisions in numerical form. This impedes communication. Numbers are easier to grasp when accompanied by some verbal explanation; managers are not mathematicians or theoretical physicists.

5. *The antimeasurement cult.* Exactly opposite to the rabid quantitator is the man who will have none of the "dehumanizing methods of the social scientists." His position boils down to the belief that nearly all important questions are important *simply because they are not amenable to quantitative answers.* Perhaps the most determined of antimeasures in executive ranks are the lawyers: the corporate counsel, the labor lawyer, the antitrust lawyer, the patent counsel. Bemused of words, capable of mastering vast amounts of verbal information and producing it upon demand, the legal counsel often succeeds in casting a spell over management in the face of what the accountant and financial expert would present as facts of high significance.[15] At many a corporate headquarters, relations between the lawyers and the accountants are like that of baboons and leopards in and around a giant tree. They frequent the same places, but enjoy at best a noisy and occasionally fatal relationship. Glib, articulate, able to use words with almost magical skills, the word-man fears and hates hard data—and often also its proponents.

Sales and marketing managers have an antimeasurement bias of major proportions when it suits their convenience. Normally this bias is more strident in expense areas than in revenue areas. Whenever the controller suggests that their expenses are slightly higher than ordinary, or perhaps even a bit extortionate, their defense is immediately to deride the importance of numbers. "You have to spend it to make it" or "We couldn't afford not to" are some examples. This stance is pure hypocrisy, of course. Rising sales figures are trumpeted forth by the same individuals.

Whatever his position in the organization, the antimeasure may be relied upon to attack conclusions based upon statistics or quantitative measurement *because* they are measurable. He will look for exceptions and offer explanations of why the meaning attributed to numbers is erroneous. Could it be that some corporation men in their hearts are at the extreme end of the antimeasurement scale like a William Buckley or a John Ciardi, whose biases are a love of *words*, pure words? They admire the language—they study and fondle it, and use it with masterful skill. From their mouths come words that scourge ignorance, ring moral gongs, sound adulation bugles, damn sin, generate enthusiasm, and inspire reverence. Each phrase is a hammer that smashes the statistic and shows the quantitator to be a dullard and boor. A gifted poet or bel-letrist is unlikely to get to the top of a corporation—unfortunately for the quality of life in the executive suite. However, management abounds with garden-variety antimeasures. When a covey of them take complete charge, as has happened in some universities, the results are typically administrative chaos, human agony, and eventual disaster. Unless persuaded to bring aboard a few accountants and others who can count the tuition income and pay the interest on the dormitory bonds, they are likely to talk themselves into bankruptcy.

Chapter 8

Don't Confuse Me
with the Facts—
My Mind Is Made Up

After managers have decided on an activity, they resist any new facts that might change their minds.

THE MISTAKES OF ILLOGIC that were discussed in the last chapter can be overcome by recognizing them and allowing for their distorting effects. Much more difficult to cope with are those failings that go unrecognized by the executive because they are rooted in his own psyche. Decision-makers are often not conscious of the biases that grow out of their backgrounds, characters, and personalities—their own drives, needs, expectations, and external demands.[1]

The director of college recruiting in a major midwestern corporation each year could foretell one action of his company president. The executive would casually drop around to the recruiter's office and tactfully suggest that he would be willing to take on, despite his extremely busy schedule, one campus recruiting trip if invited. The recruiter, being of sound self-preservation instincts, would accordingly suggest that perhaps the chief could, if his busy schedule permitted, assume personal responsibility for recruiting at his alma mater, an Ivy League school. As predictably as the coming of the crocus, the president would inform the director of recruiting within two weeks

127

that there was one outstanding candidate for whom a place should be found in the firm's management ranks: the captain of the hockey team at Good Old Ivy. It was not an astonishing coincidence that the president had captained his college hockey team. The harm was not great; in fact, a number of outstanding young men who made substantial contributions to the management rank were thus obtained. But on one occasion the boss brought back a specimen whose thinking apparatus, the recruiter concluded, had been set slightly awry, perhaps by a slap shot or butt stroke between the eyes at Hobie Baker Rink or elsewhere in the past. Despite the recruiter's gentle suggestions that this was one they might, for once, pass over, the president stoutly defended the need for the company to take up Young Master Ivy. Recognizing the strength of the emotional involvement with which he was faced, the recruiter yielded gracefully and was able to place the scarred young veteran in a position where he was responsible for giving out samples of the company product, a function which he performed moderately well.

Such developments have nothing, of course, to do with management information systems or with the logical improprieties that can sometimes muddy the handling of data. The story illustrates one of the ways in which people in high places can become emotionally attached to irrelevancies. When such a love affair with the unimportant occurs, there is little by way of more information that will modify the decision. "Don't bother me with the facts—my mind is made up" becomes more than a humorous wall decoration.

Such emotional attachments to irrelevancies by decision-makers may be classified as follows:

1. They fasten upon the big lie and stick with it.

2. They are attracted to scandalous issues and heighten their significance.

3. They press every fact into a moral pattern.

128

4. They overlook everything except the immediately useful.

5. They have an affinity for romantic stories, and find such information more significant than any other kind, including hard evidence.

6. They elevate capricious bits of information into heightened significance, and make judgments accordingly.

Emotional attachments to some institution, person, theory, or whatnot can turn the most carefully tooled management information system into nothing more than a jungle drum network insofar as logic and accuracy are concerned. The strong ties in such cases are usually with something in the executive's past and hence are an influence for conservatism. Without doubt, it is easier to form fond attachments for the old red barn at Grandfather's farm, which was the scene of many warm childhood memories, than for the new automated, scientifically designed Harvestore milk and beef production factory of the seventies. The following is an account of how each of these emotional attachments produces improprieties in logic and helps to ensure the perpetuation of the activity trap.

1. *The big lie.* In the case of the company president who made his annual spring homecoming trip to Old Ivy, the big lie was his belief that Old Ivy was somehow the fountain of all excellence, virtue, manhood, and knowledge. For anyone to have implied otherwise would have seemed to him such an affront to the truth that he would have been impelled to strike out and fire that person or at least to downgrade his promotional opportunities in the firm. The big lie is big because it looms large in decision-making.

This story is not difficult to believe—one expects that people will have biases concerning their old school ties. But somehow it comes as a surprise when, as we move on to other examples in this category, we find executives of major corporations being taken in by their own press releases. The search for images is a major concern to public relations departments these days, with large sums of money being expended on corporate images.[2] If this effort were like that of a skinny kid who bought a suit with padded shoulders to make himself resemble Dick Butkus of the Chicago Bears, the result would merely be amusing, harmless vanity. There is even a possibility that the image might become a helpful standard against which behaviors inside the organization could be rated. Kenneth Boulding has pointed out the importance of image, especially self-image, in affecting our behavior. If we have a certain image of ourselves, we are apt to behave as we think befits a person with such an image. We act as if the image were true and, as a result, the image becomes true. Similarly, when we change our image, our behavior can change if the new image is a desirable and attractive one.[3]

All of this degenerates into pure vanity when the image-seeking becomes more important than the reality. The millionaire who struck oil when he was young hires a public relations department to make him look respectable, and his employees find that they can't talk to him any more—he won't hear the truth if it doesn't fit the new self-image prepared for him by his PR adviser. In one instance, the "build-up" man lined him up for several speeches on college campuses. In an astonishingly short period he acquired the manners and style of a professor, or at least those that professors are reputed to have but usually don't: his staff meetings became "colloquia," and his board meetings were "seminars" where "issues" were discussed. An honorary degree made the man's self-image even greater. Having thus developed a vehicle for arriving at a lofty level of truth beyond that ordinarily attained by executives and never reached by those fools out on the oil rigs, he began to judge all reports from the field in the light of this higher knowledge and loftier perception. He finally went broke. His field superintendent explained it: "You just couldn't talk to the guy any more; he wouldn't hear you."

There are, of course, other sources of images which turn

into big lies. Shortly after an implement manufacturing company opened a couple of overseas branches, they announced that José, the export manager, was now "Vice-President of the International Division"; from then on all company propaganda referred to the International Division. The company logo became a terrestrial ball. Once it started seeing itself as an "International Company," it began to behave like one, in all ways except profitability. The president took trips to trade fairs in Milan and Frankfurt and reported about world economic conditions, making predictions about the admission of Britain to the Common Market and similar global issues. As this image became reinforced, more executives got bitten, and they made disastrous arrangements with foreign firms, including the acquisition of a heavy loser in Belgium. They never really learned what international business required. It took a change of presidents to get them out of the snare into which they had deluded themselves.

It is even more serious when the founder of the firm clings to the untruth that the basic character of the business is the same as when he founded it back in 1923. No amount of market research, accounting information, or new product technology data is going to make him drop the old line "on which this company was founded." What started out as a bright and shining truth is now a big lie, and worse, a dangerous one.[4]

The big flour milling companies which stuck too long to a declining market due to changes in consumer habits were often caught by founder's faith that "milling is an ancient and honorable profession."[5]

The resistance of many old-line retailers to discount stores grew out of the faith of the founders that "you can't increase your profit by cutting the prices." Meanwhile, Kresge, under a new president who was not emotionally attached to the past, grew from $300 million to $4.5 billion in annual sales through their K-Mart discount stores.

When the general officers of the military remained loyal to

horses and scoffed at tanks and when the naval staff refused to see the potentials of aircraft in naval warfare because they were attached to ships, they were demonstrating attachments to the big lie. Firmly entrenched, it epitomizes the activity trap.

2. *The scandal fallacy.* Some people simply can't resist a juicy bit of scandal. This unamazing statement is not applicable merely to the ladies' sewing circle or the residents of *Peyton Place.* Lamentably, its victims sometimes occupy high positions in business and government. Not that it is undesirable that wrongdoing should be noticed and the wrongdoer punished. The scandal fallacy arises when the possibility of a scandal, real or imagined, becomes the major test to determine the significance of received information. It is easy to see what this can do to a well-designed management information system. The process has two steps: (1) discover a moral principle or make one up; (2) condemn somebody for violation of it.

In recent years the undesirable political consequences of scandalous occurrences have been evident. The upset of the management of the Pennsylvania Railroad has been documented amply.[6] The decline and fall of Chrysler and its subsequent salvation in the hands of a reform group; the near-extinction of Ford Motor Company in 1946 and its turn-around under the founder's grandson, Henry Ford II, could be matched with other stores from corporations which showed both political machinations and the importance of controlling scandal. The Bernie Kornfeld story. Billie Sol Estes, the Guetera oil swindle which rocked some of America's most prestigious corporations, and the great electrical conspiracy of the late fifties are not forgotten by corporate directors. In 1972 the previously untarnished image of Geneen's ITT was blemished by stories of antitrust payoffs and of attempts to affect foreign policy. Tried and executed mainly in the newspapers, the case is a major reminder that scandals can reach out and touch the biggest and best.

Having some of the ethic of original sin the scandal fallacy has been assisted by the rapid growth of the accounting profession in recent years. The accountant is usually trained to work for a firm of Certified Public Accountants (CPA), which is where the majority of accounting graduates are employed when fresh out of school. There they audit books, checking to see that all funds due the firm were received, that all funds paid out were for goods actually received, and that both classes of transactions can be proved. In effect, the early apprenticeship of the accountant is as a crook-catcher. Being competent and bright young men, it would be unnatural if once in awhile they did not rejoice slightly if they could report "I got one"; in fact, it would probably be positively abnormal if they did not.

This growth has led to overstaffing in some accounting departments: most line managers at Ford agree that theirs is a monster; one large steel company has an *acre* of accountants. When times get tough in the industry generally and higher levels of management start casting an eye about for places to trim the fat in the organization, the accounting department may be tempted to find some scandal to prove their worth. The internal auditor, who is an accountant but ordinarily separate from the accounting department, likewise becomes a source of true error—and also of scandalous fallacies.

All of this audit and control is not without its uses, but it has some unintended effects as well, the most important being the production of the scandal fallacy. It assists top management in implementing its own paranoia. In the hands of a top man who has been excessively gripped by the scandal fallacy, all business in the company revolves around the secret and somewhat furtive essence, where the dirty deals are made. He often tape-records his phone conversations, hires private security firms to conduct investigations for him, and is clever at sending out "trial balloon" messages, that is, messages over an assistant's signature to gauge the effect. He is abreast of the

133

current rumors and joyously has taps into the grapevine. Apt to hire ex-FBI men for his staff, he will ask for an employee's "dossier" when he wants a personnel folder.

All of this nefarious activity, resembling wartime OSS or a bland kind of James Bond movie, would be perfectly harmless if it were not so devastating in its effect on management information systems and the processes of managerial decision-making. A proposal for something new dropped into such a machine will be engulfed, disassembled, screened through a thousand rumor mills, with its rejection usually coming in the form of dead silence, which no amount of polite budging will break.

A company thus afflicted is *not* conducive to enthusiastic generation and proposal of exciting, innovative, and perhaps risky new ideas. It's also a rotten place to work.

3. *The "angry God" syndrome.* Another form of emotional attachment which overrides logic and tests data according to a nonlogical pattern is that of the moralistic criteria of significance. That information is considered most accurate which fits most closely into a moral code close to the heart of the deciders. Like Cotton Mather's "Sinner in the hands of an angry God," each fact is weighed as to its goodness and badness.

To draw the line between judgments that are perfectly valid executive functions and those that have become a kind of moralizing priggery is difficult. Undoubtedly, executive decision-making is not automatic and systematic, but incorporates the values of the executive.[7] There are companies where it is practically tantamount to dismissal to be known to drink or have liquor on one's person, while in other firms an executive is threatened with dismissal if he doesn't participate in drinking bouts with customers. In still others, it is impossible to be hired if one has been divorced. For many others, however, it is considered to be of no concern what the employee does or doesn't do outside the office, so long as he does his work and doesn't damage the company reputation by his behavior. Information suggesting immorality is judged bad news and that which denotes morality or perhaps saintliness is considered extremely good news. But what is morality?

For corporations these days morality extends beyond personal codes of conduct to corporate responsibility as well—being a good citizen or taking part in community activities. Thus, if five young men are all performing equally well in the lesser ranks, but one is elected president of the Junior Chamber of Commerce, his value may rise faster than that of the other four with a firm where such values as community development are "good." If, on the other hand, his firm is owned by a Scrooge whose attitude is that any employee effort not wholly devoted to increasing the profit of the firm is a form of cheating, his employer may be enraged at this treachery.[8]

The most acceptable pattern for managing morals is, first, to have some and, second, to make them clear to the organization. This doesn't eliminate morals; nor does it impose the boss's. Nor should it be expected that executives will ever become value-free, decision-making machines. There are organizations that declare their sole purpose to make money yet that would, if put to a test, turn down profitable operations in many lines of human endeavor for which there is widespread demand. It is unlikely, for example, that most major corporations would enter prostitution as a business, even if it were legalized, or gambling (apart from the stock market), running sweepstakes or bingo parlors, or selling marijuana. This statement is, of course, made a priori. Nobody can tell exactly how corporations would act if all of these activities were legalized, yet it is to be expected that moral judgments will always comprise criteria for screening information. In some instances, these may be the overriding test, resulting in

135

decisions in favor of retaining the status quo, regardless of the pressures for innovation.

4. *The end-of-my-nose fallacy.* Especially prevalent among manufacturing and sales executives but not absent elsewhere is the "What will it do for me *today?*" syndrome. This is a form of myopia affecting people who must manage under extreme time pressures and who respond by putting similar time pressures on the people who work for them. If the goods aren't coming off the back end of the production line, all is lost—and the offender won't be around tomorrow. Thus, every question and every decision must be valued in terms of immediate contribution to output.

Isn't such a man a truly output-centered person? Isn't he the antidote to the activity trap? If the objectives are short-term, he may be. Certainly meeting today's schedule will require concentrated attention and quick response to anything interfering with production. Time is of the essence. In saving *time,* however, he may be generating output with no value, and resources are wasted.

Decisions of top management should not be of a short-term character. In effect, for top management to become ensnared in minute-by-minute affairs leaves the organization without a head. Even Moses learned this lesson. As described in Chapter 18 of *Exodus,* the people of Israel wandered in the wilderness without success for forty years, searching for a promised land, until Moses finally divested himself of much of the detailed decision-making. Upon the advice of Jethro, he divided the Israelites into groups of ten, clustered the tens into hundreds, and the hundreds into thousands. The small problems the people took to the leaders of their tens, the problems of the leaders of the tens went to the leaders of the hundreds, their problems went to the leaders of the thousands, and only the leaders of thousands could bring their problems to Moses.[9] Shortly afterward, the promised land was reached.

136

Presumably, prior to this reorganization, anybody could get to see Moses who, in that respect, resembled some modern company presidents who started the firm and, after it grew large, continued to be accessible for every problem, large and small.

The top manager who insists upon receiving every minute bit of information of immediate consequence is interfering in lower decisions, perhaps leaving undecided some important strategic decisions.

Asking or answering questions on the telephone, walking the floor interacting with people, checking and correcting—these are the ordinary activities of the first-line supervisor and perhaps his immediate second-level boss. To do them well calls for quick thinking, rapid decisions; the major error in decision-making is to make none. Decisions must be made fast, with the hope that most of them are correct. This description could serve as the journalistic or movie version of what a good boss looks like.

It also happens to be a horrible caricature of a top manager. The end-of-my-nose fallacy assumes that *things are being done* right. The higher-level manager must rely upon supervisors to do this, while he assures that *the right things are being done*. Even at the levels of foremen, sales managers, and middle management, more demands for mixing short and long range are becoming apparent. Jobs that call for "thinkers and doers" are more prevalent than pure management jobs. The change in managerial behavior required to attain this desired condition would seem to be some time in coming, if reports of subordinates are to be believed. If one were to commit the impropriety of trying to express an essence (see Chapter 1) from the bulk of the behavioral research which has been reported, one might say that many of today's human relations problems on the job could be solved if the boss would simply

137

get off the employee's back. This could be done without any loss of control over results, if the boss were to clearly spell out what he expects of his employees.

5. *The romantic-dramatic fallacy.* Hard facts and the management information system take a beating from another logic chopper: the romantic fallacy, or its variant, the dramatic fallacy. It adds absurd significance to facts if they fit a romantic image of the executive suite and detracts from them if they do not fit that image.

In one southern company it was for years usual to start the day with a prayer. Since this was a practice instituted by the owner, everyone, including a few agnostics who had mouths to feed, assiduously adhered to it. The rest of each day was in tune with the Quakerlike image with which it had begun: nobody smoked cigarettes or drank coffee in the office; no expletives more searing than "heck" were ever heard; tempers were cool, and smiles were plentiful. When anybody got out of line, he was never chewed out but was instead quietly admonished. What was overlooked in this idyllic milieu was that nothing ever changed. Every decision was clearly in the hands of smiling Mr. Big as he walked about extending his blessings and keeping an eye on things. Everything he saw he liked, and it was good because it was exactly the way he wanted it. There were no new product-development ideas, new office equipment wasn't introduced, and none of the newfangled accounting systems were employed. Eventually, the company began to lose money. Finally the firm was acquired by a large northern company. A new young general manager came in and ended the romantic era—and started making money.

The romantic dream fallacy takes innumerable forms. In some cases, such as that of Jack Daniels Whiskey, it has become a great advertising theme. In the case of Ford Motor Company, the advertising program, "Ford has a better idea," had the unintended side effect of spurring submissions to

138

the employee-suggestion plan. Whether or not it helped to sell more cars than General Motors is unfathomable. In General Motors an attempt to create a romantic dream with its "GM Mark of Excellence" was reported to have a good effect upon sales without an equal impact on employees. A sampling by a cynic of GM automobiles out of one plant in 1970 showed that some of these marks were put on upside down and some were pasted on askew. In one instance, when a general manager of General Motors went to receive delivery of his new car, the Mark of Excellence fell off.

Within a company this fallacy can assure that the firm will resist criticism because it has created a romantic fiction of its infallibility. The reality of the *arrogant* company is unquestionable. One can sense arrogance when first entering the premises, and it persists from top to bottom. The receptionist is cool and patronizing, and the hubris climbs from there. In conversations people on the payroll allude to the "company's prestige." This astonishes hearers who have been reading all sorts of damning things about it in the press and listening to customers rage at it and to suppliers bemoaning the fact that as a customer it is one of the world's greatest chiselers. As for changing things that need changing, of course, nothing happens.

The romantic fallacy is abetted by the physical equipment and fittings—Danish furniture, thick rugs, credenzas, a paneled conference room, or even a new modern office building—in which executives work. Executives simply get taken in by their own teakwood furniture. The effect upon interpersonal relations and decision-making of moving from a weatherbeaten and well-used building into a new tinted-glass and stainless-steel building can easily be noted. One such move physically isolated the top officers from the rest of the organization in a separate building which was connected to the main building by a two-story bridge. The bridge had glass-paneled sides so

139

that everyone's coming and going was highly visible, and it eventually became an immense source of rumors. It also divided the executives in more than physical ways. The sense of being on trial, of appearing before the gates of the mighty, of entering Vatican City was created where it had not existed before. Conversations became more stilted and stylized, the casual informality which had existed in the old beat-up downtown building having vanished. Even old cronies of the executives found themselves caught in a heartiness they didn't really feel. The major cause was the executives themselves. The richness of the architecture of the new building, the opulence of their quarters, the obvious status differences between their furniture and that of the help across the way, with the latter's plain gray steel cases and vinyl office floors, roped them all in. As one employee put it: "They are all posing for Holy Pictures."

The *dramatic* fallacy often flows out of the physical surroundings or settings in which people work. If their settings are old-shoe, comfortable, and timeworn, they fit their role to the scene. The script starts with "Aw, shucks." If it is penthouse modern and resembles the set from *Executive Suite*, the dress, the manner, and the players tend to follow suit. Decisions are made which do not *clash* with the setting.

The importance of the romantic and dramatic fallacies is that management is being treated as an art, to be performed for the aesthetic and cultural titillation of an audience.

Perhaps the most dramatic—and meaningless—example is that of the daily executive meeting of top management in each of the major airlines. Each day, usually at noon, they gather at corporate headquarters around a large table fitted with elaborate communications equipment. Each vice-president has, in addition to the familiar pad and pencils, two-way radio communication with O'Hare, Kennedy, Los Angeles International, and other major airports. First, a weather report from around the world, then a brief verbal chat with each station manager. As each reports on dollar volume, canceled flights, and similar detailed information, every vice-president grips his pencil and prays that nothing damaging to him will be said. As a dramatic performance, it rates high. This author's impression was: "My God, these people are playing a daily serial out of *Twelve O'Clock High*, featuring Gregory Peck." As a drama, it is superb. As management, it is highly expensive, quite apart from the damage it does to the organization. What can the president of the world-wide airline do with the knowledge that the baggage was tumbling on the carousel in Boston yesterday? or that a stewardess broke the heel on her shoe on the grating in Oklahoma City?

Such a drama is not without effect in operating the company. Many of the decisions at lower levels are made with a view to what they might sound like on the noon meeting wires. Which means that all of the small matters will be watched closely at the top, perhaps taking away precious time from the larger issues.

6. *The capricious information fallacy.* The final class of irrelevancies to which managers become attached is a catchall, since it is not really possible to describe all of the capricious factors that have influenced managers in judging information.

It would be easy to assume that executives are by and large less superstitious than the population at large, if for no other reason than their average educational level. But even among the educated population, there is enough superstition to make this a force to reckon with in executive decision-making. A former Prime Minister of Canada was reported never to introduce legislation unless the hands of the clock in Parliament were in a straight line, as at a quarter of three. Dozens of presidents of my acquaintance are regular horoscope-readers, and on especially crucial deals may defer things a day or two if the stars are not favorable. Of course, they aren't too open

141

about this, for it might be considered demeaning behavior for a president or vice-president. Matters of personal perquisites, personal deference—in short, matters of pomp and status—are weighed along with facts. The cheeky young engineer stands less chance of getting an appropriation than a calm, deferential one. Somehow, our expectations are that higher-level people will have, in the process of rising, purged themselves of the ordinary human failing of capriciousness. To some extent they have done so, to their lasting credit. They have learned not to be irritated because it has cost them dearly in the past. This, however, leaves a large expanse of capricious likes and dislikes which may determine which facts coming out of a management information system will be noticed and which will not.

How to Handle Attachments to Irrelevancies

It is amazingly simple to handle the other fellow's short-comings. All he has to do is stop doing it. "Even your short-comings, I can help you with if you will cooperate and realize that I am doing it for your own good. My own? You simply don't understand!" Top managers and management committees who become enmeshed in the six major fallacies require two basic curative measures.

1. *Know your biases and allow for them.* Nobody escapes biases, and it would be pointless to advise people that they shouldn't have them. Suppressed or open, they exist. The executive and its policy- and decision-making bodies would do well if they would periodically review their own decisions for evidences of bias. It is natural for mature adults to be taken in by persuasive people, to dislike scandals, and to adhere to some kind of moral code. Their experience in rising through the organization has taught them that attention to details pays off, and accordingly, they continue to do so even

142

when it is no longer productive behavior because of the lofty level they now occupy. All of us have some romantic elements, and it is said that there is some ham actor in everyone. This is equally true of superstitions, which tell us that a certain line has been "lucky" for us.

If you study your own biases, you can allow for them and not let them hurt you. It's the unconscious bias that does the most damage.

2. *Seek out independent opinions.* If you have reason to believe that your biases are affecting your decision-making, talk to some person who doesn't have an interest in the outcome. He may be a member of the board, a head of another organization or department, or an acquaintance in a noncompeting firm. A truly objective opinion is not always easily found, for many advisers have a vested interest in the outcome of the decision (*the paid adviser has an interest in continuing the relationship*). The best adviser is one who would give you his opinion candidly, even if it meant that you would not ask him anything again. The best management consultants adhere to this principle, but others may only advise in ways which will enlarge the retainer.

Chapter 9

The Money Tree Companies and Other Functionally Effective Organizations

In successful organizations more people are clear as to their objectives than in less successful organizations.

A MURAL STRETCHES ACROSS THE FRONT of the administration building of the *Instituto Tecnologío* in Monterrey, Mexico, depicting an obviously villainous serpent being stamped upon by what appears to be a group of engineers. One is told that the serpent is Ignorance, which in theory is being suppressed by Learning. After considerable study of the mural, I arrived at the conclusion that the muralist was not thoroughly persuaded that ignorance was really done for, despite the virtuous motives and currently dominant position of the engineers. After reading thus far in this book, you may be similarly disposed to conclude that ignorance is winning. Indeed it might seem that the odds against our ever becoming an orderly, rational, conscious, and human society are hopeless. Despite the foregoing catalog of errors and omissions of mere mortals, I am not so persuaded.

The evidence of hope I see for finding effectiveness in administration and management lies in the experience of those companies and administrative agencies where the antidotes for bureaucracy and the activity trap have apparently been discovered and applied well. There are certain companies that are apparently money trees, seemingly attaining what they have set out to do.

What makes a money tree company a money tree? I see seven advantages that the money tree companies have developed and exploited to their advantage.

1. They make lots of money, good times and bad, year after year; they make money where others may falter; they make it in ever growing amounts.

2. They produce more managers than lesser companies, not only enough that they have plenty themselves, but they overflow to other firms too.

3. They have heightened the importance of objectives to almost exaggerated significance in their management system and, in the process, they have played down personalities and diplomas.

4. The core of their management system is an assumption that "success means succeeding and failing means not succeeding," and that success is determined by setting objectives.

5. The money tree companies are more than efficient operators, they have effective strategic objectives, which are set prior to setting operational objectives.

6. Money tree companies get more use from staff departments than nonmoney tree companies. They manage the post-industrial men on their payroll better than less successful companies.

7. All money tree companies have big problems at one time or another, but they are capable of speed of response in their solutions.

Since these are prescriptions which can help one avoid the activity trap, or escape its clutches, let's look at each in more detail.

145

The Money Tree as a Management Academy

If, of course, the profit motive is not admired as an objective, one can hardly be expected to be wild in his enthusiasm for money tree companies, but, nonetheless, must admit that if that is their purpose, then they are successful in attaining them. ITT, under Harold Geneen, has grown from slightly over $800 million in sales to over $8 billion, with fifty-two quarters of rising earnings per share. IBM, which started under the senior Thomas Watson as a $3 million a year company, is currently producing $8 billion a year in sales, having shown a 19 percent growth rate per year for the past twelve years since Thomas Watson, Jr., took charge, with earnings per share rising even faster. General Electric will surpass $10 billion in sales at this writing, with both Ford and General Motors being generators of sales in amounts that make them prodigious, at $20 billion and $34 billion respectively.[1] The annual edition of the Fortune 500 list of companies is generally conceded to be a roster of "money trees" and, by the crude measure of money income and profit, must be considered successful. My research further points to an explanation of this success.

People in successful companies are clearer as to their objectives than in other companies which have grown large and faltered or never made it at all.

An overlooked fact is that these companies operate in such a way that they train managers to manage not only for themselves, but for others as well. Ford, for one, has not only done well by its stockholders, but has produced a surplus of managers for itself and has generated an overflow of successful presidents and officers for other companies which have, in turn, moved on even more successful operations.

146

When Zenith Radio, long a desultory performer, needed a new chief executive, they imported John Nevin, who promptly turned the company around and produced an amazing upward surge in its results. Bell and Howell, a fairly good camera company, became a money tree when it acquired Don Frey from Ford to head it. Both Boeing and North American Rockwell weathered drastic declines in sales without losing profit during the aerospace cutback under ex-Ford top management. Over forty chief financial officers of corporations started their careers under Vice-President Lundy of Ford. Robert McNamara became Secretary of Defense and is now president of the World Bank after having risen through Ford's ranks to its presidency by age forty. Tex Thornton, chairman of the $2.6 billion Litton Industries conglomerate, held his first industrial position at Ford in 1946 before departing for the West Coast where he acquired Litton Industries from Charlie Litton when it grossed less than $3 million in annual sales.

Litton, in turn, has been the producer of presidents for numerous successful organizations. George Scharffenberger, builder of City Investing from under $10 million to over a billion, is a Litton Industries dropout (LIDO). Similarly, Fred Sullivan departed Litton to head Walter Kidde, a small fire extinguisher firm in New Jersey, to turn it into a near-billion-dollar size in seven years. Walter Gray quit Litton to assume the helm at United Aircraft with the salutary effect of its becoming very profitable after years of losses or miniscule profits. Teledyne, Hunt Foods, and more than twenty others have benefited by hiring LIDOs. One of the more recent such dropouts has been Roy Ash, Litton's president, who has taken over the key position as Director of the Office of Manpower and Budget in the Nixon Administration.

General Electric, P & G, General Mills, and other money tree companies have similar records of producing more than enough managers to maintain their own momentum, at the

147

same time that they have been academies for the production of managers for other more troubled firms. It is thus possible to construct a *mainstream* of good management which reveals clearly how certain essential skills have been transmitted from one generation of managers to another. General Motors, through a generous bonus system, has been exceptional in holding on to its managers, but even here, it has provided its share of leadership to others. Ernest Breech, vice-president for twenty-one years under Alfred P. Sloan, was enticed to Ford in 1946 where he became the tutor of Thornton, McNamara, Henry Ford II, and a whole host of successful managers. What he brought with him to Ford was not secrets of styling and design or mass production, but the managerial skills learned from Alfred P. Sloan. Sloan, too, grew from a tutorial which met in the plants and offices of General Motors under Pierre Du Pont who came to Detroit in 1920 when General Motors was going broke and taught his management system to a corps of disciples before returning to his own company in Delaware. Donaldson Brown, Alfred Bradley, John L. Pratt, "Boss" Kettering, James Roche, and whole generations of executives who have directed the affairs of General Motors over the past fifty years emerged from the Du Pont-Sloan influence.[2] What were these lessons so well taught and learned by the Du Ponts, Sloans, Breeches, Thorntons, and Watsons?

They learned that success is a product of unremitting attention to purpose.

The Heightened Objective

Readers of the quickie "How to Succeed in Business" book and devotees of the "Secrets of Success" courses which abound recognize this popular formula instantly. Because it is so simple to describe and so difficult to execute, many of the more sophisticated members of large organizations brush it

148

aside. This indifference to the obvious explains the pervasive effect of the activity trap. Everyone would like to presume that explanations of complex behaviors must have a complex beginning; yet, the great organizers and founders of large organizations apparently were able to transmit the basic idea clearly. Andrew Carnegie, the Howard Hughes of his day, spent six months of each year in Europe buying technology (and interfering in British politics) and receiving reports of results against objectives. He explained his method in simple terms: "Put all your eggs in one basket and keep your eye on the basket."[3] President Abraham Lincoln stated the fundamentals of modern corporate strategy when he proposed that "If we know where we are and how we got there, and perhaps where we are trending, we may be able to control a measure of our destinies." Today, this aphorism has become the model for long-range corporate planning. Modern tools such as accounting, market research, operations research, and electronic data processing are merely extensions of this heightened principle of defining goals and reviewing results against them.

Peter Drucker, in a now famous study of General Motors in the late thirties, told its executives: "The distinctive characteristic of your organization is that everyone is clear upon his objectives. You might say that you manage by objectives."[4] This attention to objectives in far more detail than might have been imagined as being either possible or necessary then comprises the secret.

Yet, there are many diversions which have led us to take our eyes off where we are and where we are trending. The explanations for the differences between the successful managers and the unsuccessful ones and between successful companies and unsuccessful ones have abounded. Two major fallacies have predominated over the past forty years.

1. *Personality-based explanations* of why people succeed and fail were predominant shortly after World War II. The

149

popularization of Freudian theory and the rise of psycho-analysis made everyone conscious of his inner needs, qualities, and hang-ups. What better explanation than that a person should have failed than his own inner psychological properties? To succeed, simply become trustworthy, loyal, helpful, friendly, courteous, kind, and so forth. If you were neurotic, bitter, angry, sneaky, or irreverent, you naturally would fail. Dale Carnegie taught people how to win friends and influence people, and home-cooked psychology courses were sold as the key to success. Inside the large corporations, the use of psychological tests multiplied as personnel directors sought to achieve an early identification of highly potential young men.

Yet, somehow, it didn't quite track clearly. For one thing, a more intensive and measured look at executives revealed that nobody could discover a single personality trait, nor any combination of two or more, that were present in the successful and also absent in the unsuccessful. And, unless both conditions were true, being absent in the unsuccessful as well as present in the successful, the many traits one might think of would fail to discriminate good from bad. Initiative, while often present in executive suites, is more apt to be present in the ranks of the inmates of the state prison. Intelligence is sometimes high and sometimes low among the rich and successful. Thus, personality which guarantees success is a chimera. It seemed that success did not come to those who had been genetically blessed, but to ordinary people to whom something unusual had happened.

2. *The sheepskin explanation.* Equally popular and perhaps still the most prevalent explanation of executive success has been the "myth of the well-educated manager," as Sterling Livingston of Harvard has called it. When Dad came out of World War I after earning his college degree, in addition to being part of a select group which comprised only one percent of the population, he also possessed a sure-fire predictor of

150

rising high in his life's work. The degree was a ready-made selection procedure, requiring practically no thought and barely a trace of discriminatory judgment by his employer. Fifty years later his grandson graduated from college along with 30 percent of the population in his age category. Yet, the selection criteria which were required to choose who would make it to the top and who would not had not substantially improved since 1920. While the supply of college graduates had risen sharply during the five decades, the demand had matched or perhaps surpassed it. Lloyd Warner's studies in the early sixties showed that 75 percent of the chief executives of the largest companies in the United States were degree holders.[5] For many personnel managers, this was proof that a degree "predicted" success, and accordingly they altered their policies permitting only college graduates to enter managerial ranks. Within ten years they were able to study the effects of this new policy (hiring only college grads) and were pleased to discover that 100 percent of all the successful young managers promoted during the past ten years were college graduates. The Bell System refined this self-fulfilling aphorism even further. After forty years of promoting only college graduates with high grades into higher levels, they conducted a study as to who succeeded in that giant firm. They found that there was one and only one predictor of success: high grades in college. The noncollege people could rise into first-line supervision and become skilled craftsmen, but never could aspire to officer ranks by policy direction. Those who had gone to college and attained only a gentleman's grade of "C" could aspire to certain lower- and middle-management ranks. The Bell System has subsequently abandoned this policy.

The effects were to prove embarrassing for all such firms who had previously relied upon diplomas as predictors. Tensions over salaries were created when young men with no experience in the business entered directly from college at higher pay than

151

experienced old hands who had been doing the job well for years, but lacked the essential academic credentials. Social tensions inside the organization arose from the fair-haired young upstarts moving up faster than the old guard who had emerged from the educational system at an earlier time, at a lower level of credentials. The more severe effects of this discrimination system, however, showed up in an ugly discrimination against blacks, browns, Indians, Chicanos, and women who were far less likely, by reasons of culture and background, to have attained a degree. Changes in equal employment opportunity laws and more active measures on the part of the restive rejects have revealed the limits of such policy.

The Successful Person is the Successful Person

With the bankruptcy of policies which were founded upon personalities and backgrounds, what was left for the employer who was still faced with the necessity of finding able persons to manage his business? The conclusion was that: The successful manager is a manager who is successful and the unsuccessful manager is a manager who is unsuccessful. But how, for God's sake, could a hard-nosed practical manager make anything out of that?

Such a system for managing managers and managing organizations required that success be defined again and again for every person in his job in terms of renewed goals statements.

The success could thus only exist in the light of expectations which had been clearly communicated. It was the definition of ends before each period of time began that defined success, permitted it to be achieved, and comprised the criteria for judging its quantity and quality. Combined with policies and rules which served as constraints, *the objectives were the key to success.* They also comprised a functional means by

152

which the firm could constantly keep asking itself, "What are we in business for?" It was the vehicle through which ordinary people attain extraordinary things. A company or organization with goals, missions, purposes, and aims clearly in hand could then seek out responsible people and ask for their commitment to the attainment of these goals. It could tell them what was expected in terms of results; it provided the facilities and training needed to do the work required; it arranged to let people know how well they were doing in their work, and what their successes and failures had been, and rewarded them according to their accomplishments.

Strategies Before Operations

Before getting operational targets into the hands of lesser ranks, however, it proved necessary to define the long-run and strategic goals of the organization. Such thinking, which is clearly a characteristic of the money tree firms, sets the stage for the release of human energy in the pursuit of the needed success. Four major questions seem to comprise the strategic points for goals-setting and results-centered management systems in the most respected of the money tree companies.

1. *Where are we now?* The answers to this question result in a posture statement, produced annually at every major functional level of the firm, and serve to bring reality into focus before launching new ventures and new paths. Statistics such as cost accounting and market share are supplemented with judgmental statements which define the strengths, weaknesses, and major problems of the organization at that moment. For the more sophisticated, the question also encompasses the forces in the outside society in which it functions, and asks itself: What are the threats confronting us, the risks to which we are exposed, and the opportunities which lay around us?

153

Innovative behavior for the money tree firms doesn't begin with futuristic speculation, but with saturation in the present condition.

2. **What trends are discernible?** This can be answered reasonably by extrapolating what is already visible. Here such questions as "If we don't do anything differently from what we are now doing, where will we be in one, two, or five years? Do we like the answers to that question?" Extrapolation assumes that you know where you are and perhaps how you got there. It permits the operation of Odiorne's Law: "Things that do not change will remain the same." But even where there is no empirical experience on which to draw, it encourages the use of human judgment from which experimentation and risk-taking can come. Like the artilleryman who fires a couple of experimental rounds (usually smoke rounds for easy visibility) in the face of uncertainty, the strategic thinker tries a couple of tentative tests of a creative hypothesis, and then adjusts.

A key antidote to the activity trap is in timely response to outside events which require changes in objectives and in behavior.

3. **What are our new objectives?** Knowing where we are and where we are trending creates a demand for new objectives. The company that fails to ask periodically "What are we in business for?" will remain in old activities which lead to extinction—and pride is a liability. The railroads which refused to face the fact that they were really in the transportation business ended up running trains and going bankrupt. The steel companies which did not see themselves as profit-making corporations continued to make steel, avoiding new technology and losing position. Those which focused upon their purposes made money in chemicals, cement, and in products which used steel. Objectives are not to be carved in marble and

154

enshrined in cornerstones, but written on paper and embedded in men's language, to be used as criteria for making decisions and conducting the affairs of business.

4. *What are our options?* Given the facts about the situation, an extrapolation of them into consequences good or bad, and a weighing of those consequences against chosen purposes, a productive and creative management function takes over. The listing of alternatives, including a few which provide some surprises, are where the innovative skills break through the activity trap. The activity trap proposes but one option: "Do nothing new." While doing nothing on occasion may be a perfectly sensible option, for example, when you are winning—know why, and your past strategies are accelerating your rate of gain—don't tinker around. The variations of "Do nothing new" are not always as obvious; most often, they include "reorganize" or "fire somebody." During a two-year period between 1961 and 1963, over three-fourths of the largest corporations reorganized in major or minor ways. In some instances, it was a sensible realignment of the management structure to fit the new responsibilities to which people were committed. In others, it was a form of evasion of problems: "After all, with the new organization changes, we have to wait and see how things work out." Firing someone is sometimes a useful way of clearing the decks for innovation when the late-departed was a chronic blocker who simply was incapable of changing his behavior. In many instances, however, it is a convenient way of scapegoating the problem.

The *surprise* option is the best evidence that the activity trap has not achieved a death grip on the organization. It is an indication that people are still able to think the unthinkable once in awhile. In many industries and government organizations, it has become impossible for a person to have unthinkable ideas, for he jeopardizes his future in the organization by revealing his heretical thoughts.

155

The end product of a good strategy is a range of original options, including some which indicate thinking the unthinkable is permissible and desirable. It is a final bit of evidence that the activity trap has not completely mastered the organization and its people.

THE POSTINDUSTRIAL MAN IN MONEY TREE COMPANIES

The most costly manifestation of the activity trap in major corporations and government agencies is in the so-called "staff jobs." These are the nonproduction, nonselling, nonoperating positions occupied by such persons as personnel managers, traffic managers, purchasing directors, accountants, lawyers, public relations men, and the like. During the sixties, the effectiveness of such people was practically exterminated. They added to cost without a corresponding output. Some evidence of this:

The telephone companies got caught on service expansion.

The major petroleum companies got trapped in an energy crisis in the early seventies.

The automobile companies were nabbed on auto safety and emission control in the late sixties.

The steel companies were placed in an uncompetitive profit position by foreign competition in the early sixties.

Some railroads went bankrupt during the late sixties and early seventies, a just penance for their inability to change.

The Occupational Safety and Health Act caught almost everyone in violation of government standards when the act was passed in the early seventies.

The Equal Employment Act of 1964 and 1969 caught most employers without adequate preparation for integrating women and minorities into their work force.

156

Ecological and environmental laws caught many polluters completely by surprise during the early seventies.

In nearly all of these cases, there were staff experts on the payroll who had early warning signals which might have averted the most traumatic effects if suitable strategy statements and the requirement to think the unthinkable had been competently utilized. But this can hardly be charged entirely to the staff people themselves. Indeed, they are usually the most intelligent and best educated people on the payroll. The fault lies largely because top management of the firm has a *postindustrial* man on its payroll and doesn't know how to get maximum output from this capability.

Who is this postindustrial man?

Unlike the industrial man who manages men, materials, machines, money, and managers (the noted five M's taught in business school management courses), postindustrial man produces intangibles with such product categories as advice, service, information, new knowledge, and control. To attempt to manage such intangibles using the supervisory and management systems which are necessary and useful in industrial management is both unnecessary and useless. This erroneous perception of his work is the major reason staff positions have become an expensive embarrassment to many organizations. The government administrator who produces no hardware is probably the most pure postindustrial man; yet he soberly adheres to administrative practices and rules which would be sound and proper in an automobile assembly plant or a flour mill.

The new organization structure (1973) at General Electric illustrates admirably how a large organization integrates the industrial and postindustrial man into management.[6] The industrial (produce and sell for a profit) divisions are clustered in three groups. The five postindustrial functions, each headed

157

by a senior vice-president, include the nonhardware aspects of corporate administration: corporate development, corporate strategic planning, technology planning and development, corporate studies and programs, and the general counsel and secretary. Within the major groups, there are counterparts to the corporate level officers, with Strategic Business Units (SBUs) in each part which comprises an industrial business. The $10 million organization is further divided into ten groups, fifty divisions, and 166 departments—each with a responsibility for making and selling products at a profit. The postindustrial departments are designed to prevent the corporate giant from slipping into the activity trap.[7] Thus, if the appliance department becomes so enmeshed that it sees itself merely as an appliance maker and seller, an SBU will be on hand to carry it firmly through a systematic strategic analysis. While the questions asked will vary, they resemble in their essential form the four questions listed above: Where are we now? What trends are apparent or emerging? What are we in business for? What are our options?

THE IMPORTANCE OF SPEED OF RESPONSE

None of the money tree companies cited in this chapter is free of problems. General Motors has its troubles with hourly rated workers: young assembly line operators have values which suggest "I won't bust my ass for General Motors, I won't even bust it for myself" and traditional modes of supervision don't seem to work as they once did. Litton made a bargain-basement purchase of Ingall's Shipyards and has rued the day many times since for it ran into cost overruns on government contracts which bled the entire superconglomerate. IBM is currently defending itself against a Department of Justice suit which would break it up into five smaller corporations under antitrust law. ITT's Washington public relations office's blundering has produced more than its share of bad public relations for the company.

Big companies produce big problems and suffer from self-inflicted wounds, and it seems improbable that wholly problem-free operation is apt to emerge soon. Yet, sound strategic planning by wisely conceived and directed postindustrial men (formerly called "staff") who have a clear fix on their role and function in the modern corporation could alleviate the worst effects of such problems.

Even more importantly, when the house is afire, there is a necessity for rapid response on the part of people in every rank to problems once discovered. Such alacrity of response calls for operating managers and employees who are not so enmeshed in yesterday's procedure that they cannot respond. How then do people become committed to rapid response and the introduction of change to keep the company alive, vital, and self-renewing?

Chapter 10

How People Grow
at Work
Rather Than Shrink

*When people are committed to a purpose,
they grow rather than diminish.*

BLENDING THE NEEDS OF THE FIRM with the needs of the individual to develop occurs at the goal-setting stage. The organization which requires the best behavior of its people cannot obtain it solely from having a wise strategy nor an ingenious organization chart. Such response demands a commitment from those people who want to see things achieved to those whose opinion is important. A major defect in the ultralogical management system installed in the Defense Department under Secretary Robert McNamara was an assumption that the Program Planning and Budgeting System (PPBS) would be self-executing. It elicited no commitment because it was inhuman. Lower levels never understood what the system demanded of them in their position, leading to its failure and ultimate discard under subsequent administrations. Similar failures in educational programs can be observed when school boards devise elegant systems of education, only to learn several years later that they didn't work due to "the obstreperousness" of teachers and lower level academic administrators.

In the corporation where the likelihood of open defiance of orders is less likely to manifest itself, the method of malicious obedience, or filling the job description and doing no more, is present where people are not committed.

How can a firm overcome the activity trap, obtain speed of response to problems, and nurture people in the process?

SEQUEL TO THE EDSEL

Perhaps the most amazing thing about the Edsel—the now infamous auto produced by Ford, which was rejected by the customers—is not that Edsel could occur in a well-run company, it is what happened afterward that is most astonishing.

The most amazing aspect of the Edsel story is that it didn't kill innovation among successive generations of managers at Ford.

In many an organization, a business blunder of the proportions of the Edsel would have dealt a crippling blow to every new idea, large and small, for generations. Ford is a large firm, it was then sixty-five years old, with long rows of chairs filled with wise old heads who might nod sagely at every upstart with a new idea and somberly remind them, "Remember the Edsel. Remember the Edsel. Remember what happened to Krafve and Crusoe when that flopped."

Yet, with the echoes of the $300 million crash still resounding about the glass-and-steel headquarters of Ford, there arose a team of feisty young men in their thirties who took charge of the Ford Division. These innovators played a bold game which resembled "You bet your job" and restored Ford's competitive position. The vehicle was a car called Mustang, and the quarterback of the new Ford Division team was Lee

161

Iacocca, thirty-five-year-old vice-president and general manager of the Ford Division (now president of Ford).

While final approval for the new car came from an array of product committees and financial reviewers, it was Iacocca who stuck his job on the line for the Mustang. At a reported salary of $125,000 a year plus a handsome bonus almost equal to that, even if he had coasted (which many an old-timer advised), Iacocca blended strategy and operational objectives into a success story of exciting proportions.

A mere twelve years out of Lehigh University, with experience as a truck salesman, sales manager, and national manager of car and truck sales, Iacocca was elevated to the leadership of Ford's largest division at an age when many a man his age working for a utility or a bank is still an assistant supervisor in the Cupcake Junction office. For his chief engineer, he had Don Frey who was even younger, and who had joined Ford from the University of Michigan where he had been an assistant professor of Mechanical Engineering. Principal design engineer was Hans Mathias, a General Motors Tech graduate who at age fifty had been buried deep in Ford's Tech Center.

The strategy was vigorous. Take the 1963 Falcon compact, beef up the horsepower, and release a new half year model change, the '63½ Falcon. Why a half year model change, one of the rare events in the industry? To test the speed of response of the division, should the Mustang meet the Edsel's fate in the marketplace, Edsel was in part a giant fiasco because its failure was not recognized early enough. The '63½ checked the response time. In April of 1964, new coach work was added and the new model car released. Market tests on the high-performance Falcon produced in January reported that drivers were excited by the way it jumped off when the accelerator was pushed. "It's like riding a high-performance race horse" reported one user, hence the name. The strategy included an early launch of the new model, thus lengthening

162

the selling year. Two different body designs provided some options to the buyer, and also to Iacocca. If the buyer didn't like the new high rear-fender line, he could elect a fastback style.

Acceptance was immediate. After the millionth copy of the Mustang had been made and sold, making it the largest launching of a new model in the history of the industry and the industry leader for five years in a row, Ford was healthy again. Iacocca was elevated to executive vice-president of the corporation, and Frey succeeded him as division manager. Mathias was made general manager of a sizable Ford division in charge of general parts. He subsequently was promoted to executive vice-president and is now retired.

Time magazine was sufficiently impressed with the colorful Iacocca and his success story to feature his unhandsome countenance on its front page as man of the week. Inside on the business pages, an editor asked Iacocca his secret. "How do I manage?" replied Iacocca. "At the beginning of every quarter, I sit down with every manager who works for me and we talk about 'what are you going to produce for me during the coming year?' That's his commitment. During the year, I help him. At the end of each quarter, we sit down and talk about how well he is achieving his goals. At the end of the year, we pull out the same memo and talk once more. 'Here is what you said you were going to produce, how well did you do?' Then we set new goals for the coming year. That," said Iacocca, "is how I manage my division."

When the curtain went up on each period, every manager was crystal clear as to what was expected of him. He received the help he needed to get the job done. He knew how well he was doing with his work. Beyond that, he was left alone. High results produced great rewards. Low performance, in turn, could result in his being shelved, demoted, or released.

This seemingly simple explanation of Mustang is replete

with insights into a goals-centered system of management. Iacocca's statement is a crisp summary of the accumulated knowledge of Sloan, Breech, Henry Ford II, and Robert McNamara, who discovered and brought Iacocca to the top. That the pupil outdid many of his teachers is not to detract from the teachers. The rudiments of the system were taught. Iacocca's ebullient style and energetic execution merely made it work better.

Doing Right Consciously

If such discoveries of effective managerial principle had to be made over and over with each new generation of managers, the failure rate of corporations would be even higher. The lamentable rate of failures among small businesses—the average length of a corporation being estimated at seven years—can be accounted for by the fact that most small businessmen are self-selected and self-taught.[1] In contrast with such failure rates are the successes of the money tree firms which build the training of managers into successive generations through man-to-man coaching. Merely doing things right isn't enough when such coaching is needed. The high performer who does his thing unconsciously must, depending upon imitation alone, require the learner to learn every mistake by repeating it. Further, the manager who fails to coach, and teaches by example alone, ruins his pupil, for while the boss is making each mistake, he is also teaching error to his underlings.

Only the manager who operates consciously can teach what he is doing to others. To allow them to learn by imitation unaccompanied by coaching on a person-to-person basis inevitably reproduces the irrelevant and visible behaviors of chiefs rather than the essentials.

From the earliest days in E. I. DuPont, the new manager has

164

been launched in his supervisory position by being given his objectives as a preface to his assumption of a new position of responsibility. Mr. Sidney Ellis, now vice-chairman at Tenneco, Inc., a three-billion-dollar conglomerate, reports that in the early thirties he was promoted to first-line supervisor at DuPont and recalls to this day his first instructions: "Mr. Ellis, you are now a supervisor. Here are your objectives, master them!" This lesson, which he learned well, was a lesson which he, in turn, taught to many others, including a corps of company presidents.

When George Love, president of Consolidated Coal Company, was thrust into the presidency of an ailing Chrysler Corporation in 1961, his first reported words to the executive staff were: "What are we in business for?" Within a year, he had turned $40-million losses into $186 million in aftertax profits, and turned the threatened corporate giant around. When General Ed Rawlings assumed the presidency of General Mills in 1960, for several years in a deep slump, his lead question to his subordinates was identical. He reported later, after starting the food giant on an upward path in growth and profits, "If you aim for nothing, that is what you'll hit." And when General Motors Chevrolet Division felt a need to fight back against a resurgent Ford Division in the sixties, one of its responses was to bring 6,900 Chevrolet dealers back to Woodhaven, Michigan, for an intensive course in "Managing the Chevrolet Dealership by Objectives."

In 1973 a study conducted jointly by four management consulting firms, members of the Association of Consulting Management Engineers, revealed that Management by Objectives (MBO) is used by 83 percent of the leading corporations to establish specific objectives for the corporation, major functions or departments, and key individuals.[2]

Nor is this goals emphasis distinctively an American phenomenon. American books on how to manage by objectives have been translated into every language. The Japan Management Association in 1968 conducted bespectacled Japanese executives, armed with cameras and notebooks on an "MBO Tour" of this country. The English firm of Urwick and Orr, Management Consultants, has a reported thirty partners whose full-time assignment is assisting European companies get started in MBO. The British Institute of Management has conducted numerous seminars and training courses in Results-Centered Management. Over forty universities in this country now offer training courses running from two days to one week in MBO. In Canada the Department of Finance announced in 1972 that no budgets would be approved for any Canadian department unless henceforth they were accompanied by statements on objectives. During the early months of his tenure as Director of the Office of Manpower and Budget in Washington, Mr. Roy Ash personally visited twenty-one department chiefs in their offices to explain to them that without clearly stated objectives in the future, budgets would not find it easy going—a condition which was described by *National Journal* as "The government finally discovers MBO."[3]

That a bandwagon is clearly rolling is further demonstrated by the cropping up of MBO in academic research. Scholarly researchers are now cautiously sniffing about the edges of the idea. A dozen or more doctoral dissertations have proven that MBO exists, and other academic researchers have scouted it armed with questionnaire and interview—the academic behavioral scientist's means of discovering whether something really exists. The fact that it has already rolled over them and is down the road is, of course, pointless. As a lag indicator, the conduct of behavioral research has some potency.

The widespread acceptance of MBO might have been explained by pure faddism in its early stages, but after ten years has become the new orthodoxy of success for money tree firms. The persistence and expansion of goals management indicate that it has value for several groups. The first, explained in the last chapter, is that it makes money for companies; for this reason, people whose major concern is making money like it. Yet, it has among its most ardent advocates such humanistic types as the company personnel director, training expert, psychologist, or salary administrator whose major areas of concern are those dealing with people problems.

A management system which is centered around getting everyone committed to goals is thus functional and developmental. It makes money at the same time that it permits people to grow.

The success ethic itself contains the best explanation of MBO, some suggest. Eugene E. Jennings of Michigan State University, long a counselor to senior corporate executives, concludes that this success ethic for people who have enjoyed a taste of it (such as being made a junior executive) feeds upon itself and soon dominates other motivational influences.[4] Conventional autocratic methods used intuitively by weak or inexperienced managers deny such successes to people at work. For the diabolical, a formula for destroying a worker's will to succeed might be prescribed as follows:

1. Don't let people know what is expected of them, and when they persist, obfuscate and be contradictory.

2. As they work, demand high levels of activity, and when the activity is produced, be exacting, judgmental, punitive, and hostile for failure to achieve the undefined objectives.

3. Block all means of the man knowing his progress or send contradictory messages; when he is doing well, scoff at his efforts and deny any measure of achievement, especially where he might have sensed that there was some. Condone erroneous and misdirected behavior for long periods, then land hard upon him for having been a chronic foul-up.

4. Completely divorce your reward systems, such as pay, promotion, or recognition awards from achievement. Make all

167

such goodies on a random, intermittent, or even worse, upon a perfectly equal basis in which both good and bad performance are treated as being of equal worth.

THE FACE-TO-FACE TRANSACTION AS A KEY

Iacocca's description of MBO is noteworthy for its emphasis upon "sitting down and talking with each manager." When ITT was selected as one of Dun's "Ten best-managed companies," its president, Harold Geneen, similarly indicated that one of the keys to his managerial style for the giant seventy-division corporation is that "all key directions are decided after a face-to-face discussion with the key executive involved." What's so important about the obviously time-consuming practice of such dialogue?

For one thing, it avoids the ordinary chilling effect which cold memoranda and letters have in human relations. There are certain kinds of transactions where only face-to-face communication will work:

1. When the result sought is a bargain to be struck. Rarely will bargains by mail be effective. In labor relations the politicians who wrote the laws of collective bargaining wisely required that "the two parties shall meet at mutually convenient times and places and there shall be offer and counteroffer." To refuse to enter into such a close relationship is deemed to be "refusal to bargain" in the law.

2. Conflict resolution is another circumstance that demands face-to-face contact for success. University professors and government bureaucrats are renowned for their ferocious exchanges of letters designed to prove another wrong, and thus, settle the conflict "once and for all" with a devastating epistle. The consequence is, of course, ordinarily as soothing as a hand grenade in a telephone booth. It gets noticed, but when the dust and fumes have settled generally produces an even more violent ex-

plosion in retribution. Among the things it fails to do is resolve any disagreements, for harmonious relations come only between people who are in personal touch with one another.

3. Changing behavior which is already under way and gaining momentum requires a personal word, a human touch, which pierces through the inertia, permits a slowing down and halting before the direction is reversed.

On the favorable side, written notes of commendation, appreciation, praise, or gratitude will have few adverse effects in interpersonal relations. Apparently, we get such sparse allocations of these messages that we'll take them any way they fly.

Since the goal-setting process often involves all three of the potentially disruptive classes of transactions between people, a written memorandum system of defining goals simply won't work and may produce more mischief than constructive action. The boss may be required to bargain with key employees, such as his most productive salesman or chief engineer, especially if the subordinate is an expert in something about which the boss knows little. The goal-setting process may uncover disagreements which need resolution. Of course the entire process is aimed at changing behavior in many man-boss discussions. Accordingly, it is predictable that by omitting this face-to-face discussion and saving time through an exchange of memoranda will disrupt rather than develop the relationship, and performance will lag.

QUALITY—NOT QUANTITY—OF PERSONAL CONTACT

Having established the necessity for face-to-face contact in the goals-setting process, it might be conceived that an undesirable suffocating kind of relationship would be produced. This conception is far from the case. The learning by lower-level managers from higher-level managers is not being pressed into a kind of group encounter for hours on end, day in and

169

day out. The quantity of contact between the teacher and learner must be strictly controlled. The men who worked for Sloan and learned the essence of his managerial skill were often separated from him by distance, by time lags in their contacts, and by a certain aloofness on his part that barred a cloying kind of supervision.

The key to the teaching of management lies more in the quality of what occurs when two persons are in contact than in a simple enlargement, or frequency of the contact. The division manager for Litton Industries who caught the lessons from Tex Thornton and Roy Ash, in fact, often had only infrequent personal contacts, but the quality of what occurred in these sessions (called "opportunity sessions") accounts for the growth of a host of highly successful LIDOs. The seventy division managers in General Electric who learned their managerial trade under President Ralph Cordiner were not by any stretch of the imagination "buddies" of the top man.

What makes for a quality contact out of which subordinates grow and learn the best skills of the top man?

1. The contacts deal with goals and results. While the subject of methods and activities is not ignored by any means, the primary purpose of the face-to-face relationship lies in their almost spartan control over irrelevancies and their painfully detailed expositions and discussions of objectives, and analysis of actual results as compared with those objectives.

2. The objectives themselves are treated with care and are expanded upon until clarity and agreement are complete. The delegation of results expected is as complete as human judgment and communication skill will allow, and the assessment of results is meticulously compared with the original goals.

3. The purpose of the discussions is less apt to be judgmental than affirmative, optimistic, forward-looking, and problem-centered. Discussions of "your strengths and weaknesses" are far less likely to be on the agenda than discussion of "how could we do an even better job in the future?"

170

4. The discussion is not what Eric Berne refers to as "Parent-Child" discussions, in which the boss serves *in loco parentis,* issuing advice and admonitions. Rather, they resemble Berne's Adult-Adult relationship. Two grownups strike bargains, and mutual commitments are made. The subordinate makes promises to attempt to produce certain outcomes in the future, and the boss, in turn, is committed to certain supportive and helpful behaviors.[5]

5. Group meetings, such as board meetings, task forces, and committees likewise concentrate upon goals, results, and mutual commitments. Unlike many "staff meetings" which concentrate endlessly upon activities, with the least relevant information occupying the greatest period of time, the groups focus upon target aims and very specific objectives. When people are stuck, or the path is unclear, the activity required is planned, not as a means of suppressing nor controlling members, but of clearing obstacles, providing shared knowledge, and stimulating innovation through the process of suggestion and—a much overworked word—synergy.

THE GROWTH OBJECTIVE—AN EXPLODED DIAGRAM

Good objectives should have a stretching effect upon the person who makes commitments to attain them. Certainly there is little benefit in setting forth in writing a group of things which the writer would have done anyway, even if he hadn't written them down. It merely proves he is a lucid writer, not necessarily a doer. Nor should the memoranda which confirm agreements made in face-to-face discussion be excessively lengthy. "I spend so much time writing down what I am going to do, or have done, and what went wrong, that I don't have time to do anything" is a most legitimate complaint of one subordinate. Output descriptions can be brief. Activity statements can be endless.

The objective which has the highest motivational effect is

that which is innovative and creative in nature. It calls for the best abilities of the person, his cumulative experience, and his wit and wisdom in manipulating those memories into new and unique creations. Psychologist Abraham Maslow has suggested that "self-actualization" is the ultimate in motivation, for it permits the person to express the best of his abilities. In reaching an ego ideal, and then following it by enlarging that ego ideal and achieving it again, a person grows. The miracle of human behavior and the human personality is that the number of such steps which can be taken without exhausting its limits has not been discovered. The ultimate in success for an individual, Maslow proposed, was a "peak experience" in which all of a person's efforts and talents had been combined to attain an exciting new output.

That a person living in a world of pedestrian work must also define the routine and maintenance goals of his job is no denial of the importance of the innovative goal. Indeed, unless he delivers the ordinary commitments expected of him, he cannot retain his position to improve things and introduce changes to the ordinary. Thus, the goal which stretches a person includes some responsibility for maintenance objectives. Too many bosses, however, limit life at work solely to such maintenance goals, thus deliberately and consciously denying the growth objectives.

This emphasis upon growth and development of subordinates on the part of bosses and administrators is more than a simple device or gimmick for getting ahead or making money. It is rooted in the best of the new scientific findings about man and his behavior. The boss who attends solely and doggedly to activity control, the maintenance of the status quo, and the prevention of error perpetuates a kind of pathology-centered theory of management. The boss who fails to act aggressively in his administrative practices to exploit the potential for growth of the people under him sees all deviations

172

from normality as an aberration which must be cured as if it were a form of crime, delinquency, mental illness, if not a moral weakness. He applies an unwitting Freudian therapy to stamp out the natural weaknesses and sins of subordinates. The activity-centered manager sees growth and change tendencies only as forms of abnormality which must be put down severely.

A goals orientation demands that healthy behavior and its development be centered around growth toward loftier levels—a concept more akin to Jung than Freud. Jung sought to understand man in the perspective of his health, not of his neuroses. While Freud was more concerned about treatment through emphasis upon subconscious drives, Jung emphasized the values of people turning their passions outward and concerning themselves with higher, perhaps even nobler, aims and aspirations.

The modern boss who would develop people and make more money or reach higher levels of achievement for his organization draws too on Alfred Adler, who saw man not as an unhealthy neurotic, but as a healthy person who develops goals that are primarily social. For Adler, the primary motivation was a striving for personal superiority and achievement, which he declared was innate in humans and accounted for a great "upward drive. . . ." For the manager who is enmeshed himself and a great enforcer of the activity trap, there are numerous mental health implications in change. It moves his attitudes and behavior toward those working under him from one of preventing aberrations to enabling and facilitating growth in mental health through ever-rising aspirations. These aspirations are not merely for the mechanical substances such as increased pay or more power, but for higher levels of attainment and contribution. Carl Rogers, a contemporary psychologist, suggests that the innermost core of man's nature, the deepest layers of his personality, the base of his animal

173

nature, is positive in character. It is basically socialized, forward-moving, rational, and realistic.[6] In all of these, there is corroboration from Dr. William Glasser who rejects conventional psychiatry and the concept of mental illness, but replaces it with what the patient is doing *and intends to do*. The words *responsibility* and *commitment* which underlie the findings of Glasser, Allport, Rogers, Maslow, and Frederick Herzberg begin from the assumption of goals—and not merely maintenance goals, but growth goals. The steeper the incline of aspiration and the higher the goal, the greater the possibility of individual growth.

Life on an Inclined Plane Upward

How does such a set of goals produce a life lived on an upward- and forward-moving direction? The content of the goals statements themselves has much to do with growth-centered goals.

For one thing the basic character of the strategic goal "Am I doing the right things?" is satisfactory in terms of the values of the aspirant. The same skills of group leadership that serve the platoon leader of infantry in Vietnam might be applied to teaching in a school for mentally retarded children, with due regard for some differences. Yet the purposes of the latter could easily be seen by the person as ennobling, while the former is seen as degrading. A manager of my acquaintance switched companies. He had been director of engineering in a company making slot machines. In his new position, he applied the same talents to producing environmental control and air purification equipment. "I take the kids out for a drive on Sunday and drive past the plant with pride now. Before, I used to avoid telling them what I made. I just told them that I was an engineer in a factory." A pharmaceutical engineer may work on nerve gases or on antibiotics which save thousands of lives. Choosing the "right things to do" to reduce

174

guilt and hesitancy becomes a primary step in the goal-setting process.

People who work, my experience shows, are often hungry for some inkling of a more important meaning to their work. As a frequent speechmaker at conventions and conferences of business executives and professional groups, I have found that an unfailing surge of popular acceptance, bordering almost on adulation, follows a speech when I do a bit of research on their work and find something of importance to report to them. "There is a bigger meaning to what you are doing in your work as a ————." Fill in the blanks and verify it with details, however sparse, and I'm washed in a warm wave of grateful applause at the end. Tell a plumbing contractor that he is a dispenser of good health and sanitation, and he warmly clasps you to his heart. Treat him like a wallower in filth, and he'll charge you $15 an hour. Tell a farm equipment manufacturer that he is helping to feed the hungry of the world, and he is almost moist in his affection for you.

Immediate goals statements also should have some validity in pointing up growth possibilities. Stated another way, goals should be worded to comprise an ascending scale of excellence. This is possible by breaking all immediate individual goals statements into three classes: the regular and routine outputs which are to be produced; the problems which are to be solved; and ultimately the objectives which improve everything. Normally, as a scale of excellence, these three classes of goals are a yardstick for determining growth potentials in the day-to-day job.

The person who achieves all of his ordinary responsibilities is an ordinary performer and is entitled to the same job at the same pay for another year. He is not growing, but is merely time-serving. He may, on the other hand, do them because the routines also provide him access to other more interesting and developmental opportunities.

The person who performs his regular duties faithfully has

175

grown in capability when he proves that he can see problems that others may have overlooked and can solve them when others have failed.

The person who does his routines and solves problems with aplomb and skill can grow even more when he sees new opportunities within the routines and problems, and is committed to exploiting such opportunities.

The man who works in a climate where everyone knows that anything being done could be done better, perhaps cheaper, safer, or with greater dignity to people, will surely find that there is no one best way. His is the roving eye which sees opportunities for innovation in every existing system, product, work flow, and method. With such freedom to look, he will surely find opportunities everywhere, and life becomes a regular series of projects which move from thing to thing, place to place, job to job, all on a more elevated scale than the previous one.

NOTES

1: THE ACTIVITY TRAP

1. Stafford Beer, *Cybernetics and Management* (New York, Wiley, 1959). See also Donald G. Malcolm, Alan J. Rowe, and Lorimer F. McConnell, *Management Control Systems* (New York, Wiley, 1960).
2. "The Logic of Hegel," *Encyclopedia of Philosophical Sciences* (New York, Oxford University Press, 1929).
3. Kenneth Boulding, *The Organizational Revolution* (New York, Harper & Brothers, 1953).
4. Norbert Wiener, *The Human Use of Human Beings: Cybernetics and Society*, 2d ed. rev. (Garden City, N.Y., Doubleday, 1954).
5. For one of the most important applications see Charles J. Hitch and Roland N. McKean, *The Economics of Defense in the Nuclear Age* (Cambridge, Harvard University Press, 1960).
6. Cyril N. Parkinson, *Parkinson's Law* (Boston, Houghton-Mifflin, 1957) is a popular explanation. More research-based is Herbert A. Shepard, "Nine Dilemmas in Industrial Research," *Administrative Science Quarterly* (December, 1956), p. 295.
7. For a discussion of criteria under results-centered management see Chapter 12 in George S. Odiorne, *Personnel Administration by Objectives* (Homewood, Ill., R. D. Irwin, 1971).
8. Peter Drucker's germinal report on his studies at General Motors in the early 1940's, culminating in his *The Practice of Management* (New York, Harper & Brothers, 1954) was among the first of many to arrive at this conclusion.
9. "Business Week Indices 1960-1973," *Business Week*.
10. Robert Townsend, *Up the Organization* (New York, Knopf, 1970) is a set of observations from an experienced executive which in large part concurs with the damage from activity-centered management.

11. Theodore Levitt, "Marketing Myopia," *Harvard Business Review* (July-August, 1960).
12. John G. Hutchinson, *Management Strategy and Tactics* (New York, Holt, Rinehart and Winston, 1971).
13. Several studies on the small business and its management define this process. See Louis L. Allen, *Starting and Succeeding in Your Own Small Business* (New York, Grosset & Dunlap, 1968). See also a research report by Orvis F. Collins and David G. Moore, *The Enterprising Man* (East Lansing, Michigan, Bureau of Business and Economic Research, Graduate School of Business Administration, Michigan State University, 1964). For his ideology see John H. Bunzel, *The American Small Businessman* (New York, Knopf, 1962).
14. K. Strone and A. Clark, *Law Office Management* (St. Paul, West Publishing Co., 1974).

2: The People-Shrinker

1. Frederick Herzberg, *Work and the Nature of Man* (Cleveland, World Publishing Co., 1966) calls people "instrumental men" when engaged in forced activity without meaning to them.
2. Edwin J. Thomas and Alvin Zander, "The Relationship of Goal Structure to Motivation Under Extreme Conditions," *Journal of Industrial Psychology*, 15 (Autumn, 1959).
3. Norman R. F. Maier, R. L. Hoffman, J. J. Hooven, and W. H. Read, *Superior-Subordinate Communication in Management*; Study no. 52 (New York, American Management Association, 1961).
4. Rensis Likert, *New Patterns of Management* (New York, McGraw-Hill, 1961).
5. Chris Argyris, *Personality and Organization* (New York, Harper & Brothers, 1957).
6. Charles R. Walker and Robert H. Guest, *The Man on the Assembly Line* (Cambridge, Harvard University Press, 1952).
7. David C. McClelland, *The Achieving Society* (Princeton, N.J., Van Nostrand, 1961).
8. Thomas and Zander, *loc. cit.*
9. Herbert Meyer, Emanuel Kay, and John R. P. French, "Split Roles in Performance Appraisal," *Harvard Business Review* (January-February), p. 123.

178

10. Robert J. House and Alan C. Filley, *Managerial Process and Organizational Behavior* (Glenview, Ill., Scott, Foresman, 1969), p. 311.
11. Eugene E. Jennings, *The Executive in Crisis* (New York, McGraw-Hill, 1972).

3: HOW REALITY BECOMES INVISIBLE
   TO THE BOARD OF DIRECTORS

1. Myles L. Mace, *Directors:Myth and Reality* (Boston, Harvard Business School, 1971).
2. For a discussion of the merits of insiders versus outsiders see J. Keith Louden and Joseph M. Juran, *The Corporate Director* New York, American Management Association, 1966.
3. Peter Vanderwicken, "Change Invades the Boardroom," *Fortune* (May 1972), p. 156.
4. Joseph Daughen and Peter Binzen, *The Wreck of the Penn Central* (Boston, Little, Brown, 1971).
5. In 1972 numerous church bodies voted to use their shareholdings in companies operating in South Africa to compel those corporations to put pressure upon boards to withdraw. In August 1972 the World Council of Churches urged some 300 member churches to follow suit. *New York Times,* August 23, 1972.
6. *New York Times,* August 17, 1972.
7. Two differing versions appear in Otto Friedrich, *Decline and Fall* (New York, Harper & Row, 1970) and Matthew J. Culligan, *The Curtis-Culligan Story* (New York, Crown Publishers, 1970).
8. R. Sheehan, "Coal Man at Chrysler (G. H. Love is Chairman of auto company and Consolidation Coal of Pittsburgh)," *Fortune* (September, 1962), pp. 102-107.
9. Peter Drucker, *The Practice of Management* (New York, Harper & Brothers, 1954).
10. The many implications of this separation of management from ownership have been more fully explored. See Adolf A. Berle and Gardiner C. Means, *The Modern Corporation and Private Property* (New York, Macmillan, 1933) or Edward S. Mason, *The Corporation in Modern Society* (Cambridge, Harvard University Press, 1959).

11. Clarence B. Randall, *The Folklore of Management* (Boston, Little, Brown, 1961).

12. Roy Heath, *The Reasonable Adventurer* (Pittsburgh, University of Pittsburgh Press, 1964).

4: THE END OF MOTIVATION

1. Bernard Berelson and Gary Steiner, *Human Behavior: An Inventory of Scientific Findings* (New York, Harcourt, Brace & World, 1964).

2. This is sometimes called "classical" management theory and is identified with Frederick W. Taylor, *The Principles of Scientific Management* (New York, Harper & Brothers, 1911).

3. Robert L. Heilbroner, *The Worldly Philosophers* (New York, Simon and Schuster, 1953).

4. Herbert Marcuse, *One Dimensional Man* (Boston, Beacon Press, 1964). See also Herbert Marcuse, *Eros and Civilization* (Boston, Beacon Press, 1955).

5. George S. Odiorne, *Management by Objectives* (New York, Pitman, 1965).

6. See David C. McClelland, *The Achieving Society* (Princeton, N.J., Van Nostrand, 1961), and Chalmers L. Stacey and Manfred F. DeMartino, eds., *Understanding Human Motivation* (Cleveland, World Publishing Co., 1965).

7. Abraham Maslow, *Motivation and Personality* (New York, Harper & Brothers, 1954). See also his *Eupsychian Management* (Homewood, Ill., R. D. Irwin, 1965).

8. Rensis Likert, *New Patterns of Management* (New York, McGraw-Hill, 1961).

9. B. F. Skinner, *Beyond Freedom and Dignity* (New York, Knopf, 1971) is considered the leading theoretician of environmental effects upon behavior.

10. John Kenneth Galbraith, *The New Industrial State* (Boston, Houghton-Mifflin, 1967).

11. Frederick Herzberg, Bernard Mausner, and Barbara Snyderman, *The Motivation to Work* (New York, Wiley, 1959).

5: WHY MOST PROBLEMS DON'T GET SOLVED AND MANY GET WORSE

1. Herbert A. Simon, *The New Science of Management Decision* (New York, Harper & Row, 1960).

2. Joseph M. Juran, *Managerial Breakthrough* (New York, McGraw-Hill, 1965).

3. Charles D. Kepner and Benjamin B. Tregoe, *The Rational Manager* (New York, McGraw-Hill, 1965).

4. Bertrand Russell, "On the Notion of Cause," *Mysticism and Logic* (New York, Longmans, 1918) was considered rather heretical when he first attacked causes as a useful law of philosophers. William P. Montague, *The Ways of Knowing* (New York, Macmillan, 1958) suggests that causality has no *reality*, a point of importance in this book.

5. Frederick E. Croxton, Dudley J. Cowden, and Sidney Klein, *Applied General Statistics*, 3d ed. (Englewood Cliffs, N.J., Prentice-Hall, 1967).

6. Irving M. Copi, *Introduction to Logic* (New York, Macmillan, 1953).

7. William Lloyd Warner and J. Abegglen, *Big Business Leaders in America* (New York, Harper & Brothers, 1955).

8. Alfred P. Sloan, *My Years with General Motors* (Garden City, N.Y., Doubleday, 1964).

9. Richard C. Hodgson, Daniel J. Levinson, and Abraham Zaleznik, *The Executive Role Constellation* (Boston, Harvard Business School, 1965).

10. Norman R. F. Maier and John J. Hayes, *Creative Management* (New York, Wiley, 1962) deals with some of the fine points of group problem solving.

11. "A. D. Little's General Takes Full Command," *Business Week* (November 27, 1971), p. 24.

12. David W. Miller and Martin K. Starr, *Executive Decisions and Operations Research* (Englewood Cliffs, N.J., Prentice-Hall, 1960).

13. S. Ramo, "Can Management Be Made Automatic?" Research Report, American Management Association, 1954.

6: WHEN THE FACTS GO INTO HIDING

1. *New York Times*, August 7, 1972.

2. Harry Levinson, *The Exceptional Executive* (Cambridge, Harvard University Press, 1968).

3. Fred Fiedler, "The Effect of Intergroup Competition on Group Member Adjustment," *Personnel Psychology* (Winter 1963).

4. Bernard Berelson and Gary Steiner, *Human Behavior; An In-*

ventory of Scientific Findings (New York, Harcourt, Brace & World, 1964).

5. *Business Week* (July, 1972).
6. *New York Times* (November 24, 1971).
7. Robert Heller, *The Great Executive Dream* (New York, Delacorte Press, 1972).
8. World Federation of Mental Health, *Cultural Patterns and Technical Change,* ed. Margaret Mead (New York, New American Library, 1955).

7: THE INFORMATION OVERLOAD

1. Alfred P. Sloan, *My Years With General Motors* (Garden City, N.Y., Doubleday, 1964).
2. Russell Ackoff, *A Concept of Corporate Planning* (New York, Wiley Interscience, 1970).
3. Joseph M. Juran, *Managerial Breakthrough* (New York, McGraw-Hill, 1964).
4. Lester R. Bittel, *Management by Exception* (New York, McGraw-Hill, 1965).
5. George S. Odiorne, *Management Decisions by Objectives* (Englewood Cliffs, N.J., Prentice-Hall, 1969).
6. William D. Guth and Renato Tagiuri, "Personal Values and Corporate Strategies," *Harvard Business Review* (September-October, 1965), p. 123.
7. Jan Christiaan Smuts, *Holism and Evolution* (New York, Macmillan, 1926).
8. Robert A. Goldwin, ed., with Charles A. Nelson, consultant, *Toward the Liberally Educated Executive* (White Plains, N.Y., Fund for Adult Education, 1957).
9. Juran, *op. cit.*
10. Charles D. Kepner and Benjamin B. Tregoe, *The Rational Manager* (New York, McGraw-Hill, 1965).
11. Russell Ackoff, *op. cit.*
12. *Journal of the Academy of Management, passim.*
13. Rensis Likert, *New Patterns of Management* (New York, McGraw-Hill, 1961). See also Abraham Maslow, *Motivation and Personality* (New York, Harper & Brothers, 1954) and Harry Levinson, *The Exceptional Executive* (Cambridge, Harvard University Press, 1968).

14. George S. Odiorne, "The Limitations of Operations Research," *Personnel Policy* (Columbus, Ohio, Merrill, 1963).
15. Walter Mahler, *Journal of the ASTD* (May 1972). A consultant on MBO, Mahler has stated that counsel is the most difficult occupation from which to obtain cooperation in specific definition of objectives.

8: Don't Confuse Me With the Facts—
My Mind is Made Up

1. Harry Levinson, *Emotional Health in the World of Work* (New York, Harper & Row, 1964).
2. George S. Odiorne, "The Great Image Hunt: A Search for Corporate Objectives," *Michigan Business Review* (October-November 1967).
3. Kenneth E. Boulding, *The Image: Knowledge in Life and Society* (Ann Arbor, University of Michigan Press, 1956).
4. See T. Levitt, "Marketing Myopia," *Harvard Business Review* (July-August, 1960).
5. Eugene E. Jennings, *The Mobile Manager* (East Lansing, Mich., Bureau of Industrial Relations, University of Michigan Business School, 1967).
6. Joseph Daughen and Peter Binzen, *The Wreck of the Penn Central* (Boston, Little, Brown, 1971).
7. William D. Guth and Renato Tagiuri, "Personal Values and Corporate Strategies," *Harvard Business Review* (September-October, 1965), p. 123.
8. Chris Argyris, *Personality and Organization* (New York, Harper & Brothers, 1957).
9. Leon Uris, *Exodus* (Garden City, N.Y., Doubleday, 1958), Chapter 18.

9: The Money Tree Companies and Other
Functionally Effective Organizations

1. "Fortune's Directory of the 500 Largest Industrial Corporations," *Fortune* (May 1973), p. 220. The list is further scrutinized in "Who Did Best and Worst Among the 500" on p. 242.
2. George S. Odiorne, "Is There a Management Establishment?" *Michigan Business Review* (November, 1970), pp. 12-18.

3. Joseph Frazier Wall, *Andrew Carnegie* (New York, Oxford University Press, 1970).

4. See Peter F. Drucker, *The Concept of the Corporation* (New York, John Day, 1946, 1972) and his *Managing for Results* (New York, Harper & Row, 1964).

5. William Lloyd Warner, "The Corporation Man," in his *The Corporation in the Emergent American Society* (New York, Harper, 1962).

6. "GE's Jones Restructures His Top Team," *Business Week* (June 30, 1973), p. 38.

7. *Ibid.*

10: How People Grow at Work Rather Than Shrink

1. John H. Bunzel, *The American Small Businessman* (New York, Knopf, 1962).

2. "The Thirteen 'Most Popular' Management Techniques," *Administrative Management* (June, 1973), p. 26.

3. "OMB's Management Team to Review Agencies Programs," *National Journal* (June 2, 1973).

4. Eugene E. Jennings, *The Executive in Crisis* (New York, McGraw-Hill, 1972).

5. Eric Berne, *Games People Play* (New York, Grove Press, 1964).

6. This basic approach to psychology is described in Frank Goble, *The Third Force* (New York, Grossman Publishers, 1970).

INDEX

Academy of Management, 121
Achievement, removal of
    obstacles to, 71–76
Ackoff, Russell, 116, 117
Activity cult, 8
Activity trap
  adverse effects of, 27–29
  alternatives to, 22–23
  antidote to, 136, 154
  applied to
    the family, 5, 16–19
    governments, 4, 19–21
    hospitals, 4
    school systems, 4
    social clubs, 4
  bankruptcy, caused by, 8
  behavior of personnel, caused
    by, 10–11
  board room, in the, 50
  civil servants in, 21
  concept of, 6
  costly manifestation of, 156
  death grip of, 155
  emotional attachment, factor
    in, 7, 13
  epitome of, 132
  job descriptions, reinforcer of,
    11, 69
  lamentable outcome of, 13
  life in, 30–31
  Management Information
    Systems, part of, 115
  manager, enforcer of, 173
  overcoming, factors in, 23
  pernicious effects of, 9
  pervasiveness of, 9, 20, 149
  prescriptions for avoiding, 145
  problem-solving, reinforcer of,
    79, 80
  productive ability, effects on,
    10
  shrinking effect on, on people,
    9, 24–28
  small businesses, effects on,
    14–16
  supervisor-subordinate
    relationships in, 8, 28
Adler, Alfred, 173
Airline management, 140–141
American Management
    Association, 118
Anthony, Dr. E. James, 17
Antimeasurement cult, 125–126
Aristotle's syllogism, 2
Ash, Roy, 147, 166, 170
Association of Consulting
    Management Engineers,
    165

Bankruptcy, 8, 30, 126, 156

185

Bausch and Lomb, Inc., 110
Behavior patterns, 10–11,
    28–29, 73
  board of directors, 46–60
  changing, 169
  complex, 149
  corporate image, effect on,
    130
  employee, 134
    fallacies of, 67–68
  goal-centered, 71
  innovative, 154
  managerial, 73, 74, 137, 173
    supportive, 171
  Pavlovian stimulus-response,
    theory of, 74
  psychological, 172, 173
Behavioral research, 137, 166
  scientists, 35, 66, 87, 121
Bell and Howell Co., 147
Bell Telephone System, 101,
    151
Berne, Eric, 171
Black businesses, 22
Board of Directors
  as adventurers, 60–62
  behavior patterns of, 46–60
  of Curtis Publishing Co., 45
  decision-making, fallacies in,
    52–60
  election of a president by,
    44–45
  female representation on, 43
  under fire, 41–45
  ideal, how to build and
    maintain, 60–63
  individual director, influence
    of, 48–50
  isolation of, 50–52

minority-race representation
    on, 43–44
  objectives, role in setting,
    45–48
  of Penn Central Railroad, 42
  reality, loss of, 39–63
  reform of, 62–63
Boeing Company, 94, 147
Boulding, Kenneth, 2, 115, 130
Bradley, Alfred, 148
Breech, Ernest, 148, 164
British Institute of Manage-
    ment, 166
Brown, Donaldson, 148
Buckley, William, 126
Burlington Northern Railroad, 49
Business success, 148–159
  through innovation, 154–155,
    176
Butkus, Dick (Chicago Bears),
    130

Canadian Department of
    Finance, 166
Carnegie, Andrew, 149
Carnegie, Dale, 150
Case, J. I., 62
Certified Public Accountants
    (CPA), 133
Chamber of Commerce, Junior,
    135
Change, resistance to, 8–9, 13,
    15, 50, 51, 131
Chicago Bears, 130
Chrysler Corporation, 45, 57,
    62, 132, 165
Churches, activity-centered,
    21–22
Ciardi, John, 126
City Investing Co., 147

186

Emotional attachments in
decision-making,
127–132
Employees
behavior of, 134
children, viewed as, 67
competence of, 33
compliant, 69
goals for, 65
relief from, 18, 23
growth of, individual,
167–176
hostile, 69
images, fallacies of, 67–68
immature, 32
motivational influence on, 64
payoffs, motivational, 76
relations with, 123, 124
stereotyping, result of, 66
uncommitted, 33
Equal Employment Act, 156
Estes, Billy Sol, 132
Ewing, L. S., 107
Executive success
explanations for, 148–153
statistical studies of, 88
Executive Suite, 140
Exodus (Uris), 136

Fact-gatherers, comments on, 113
Facts
elusive nature of, 103
emotional resistance to,
127–143
hidden, 102–113
identification of, 104
Chicken Little fallacy,
105–107
figure-eight indictment,
111–112

ghost proof, 109–110
hot potato proof, 110–111
irrelevant evidence,
108–109
reversible evidence,
107–108
Federal Government, 19–21
Fiedler, Fred, 107
Ford, Henry, Sr., 92
Ford, Henry, II, 132, 148, 164
Ford Motor Company, 115,
132, 133, 138, 146, 147,
148, 161, 165
Edsel, 161
Falcon, 162
Mustang, 162
Forest Produce Industry
Conference, 81
Fortune 500 list, 146
Freud, Sigmund, 173
Freudian theory, 150, 173
Frey, Don, 147, 162, 163
Friedman, Milton, 91

Galbraith, John K., 65, 75, 76,
77
Gardner, John, 37
Gavin, James A., 97
Geneen, Harold, 132, 146, 168
General Electric Company, 34,
35, 54, 60, 146, 147,
157, 170
Strategic Business Units of,
158
General Mills, 147, 165
General Motors Corporation,
34, 44, 60, 92, 114, 139,
146, 148, 158, 162
Chevrolet Division of, 165
George, Henry, 91

190

United States Government,
19–21
Urwick and Orr (management
consultants, Britain),
166

Vance, Stanley, 60
Vartan, V. G., 110
Vatican City, 140
Veblen, Thorstein, 15
Veterans' Administration
(U.S.), 21

Veterans' hospital, expenditure
for, 124

Warner, Lloyd, 88
studies of, 88, 89, 151
Watson, Thomas, Sr., 146
Watson, Thomas, Jr., 146
Weyerhauser Timber Company,
81
Wittgenstein, Ludwig, 2
World Bank, 147

Zenith Radio Corporation, 147